Needlepoint Designs
From Oriental Rugs

Needlepoint Designs From Oriental Rugs

GRETHE SORENSEN

Drawings by the Author
Photography by Lloyd Rule and Richard Baume

CHARLES SCRIBNER'S SONS / NEW YORK

This book is dedicated to Julian Haas,
who made me believe I'm an artist.
He started it all.

Library of Congress Cataloging in Publication Data

Sorensen, Grethe.
  Needlepoint designs from oriental rugs.

  Bibliography: p.
  1. Canvas embroidery—Patterns. 2. Rugs,
Oriental.   I. Title.
TT778.C3S68   746.44'2041   80-17907
ISBN 0-684-16622-4   AACR1

This book published simultaneously in the
United States of America and in Canada—
Copyright under the Berne Convention.

1 3 5 7 9 11 13 15 17 19 Q/C 20 18 16 14 12 10 8 6 4 2

Printed in the United States of America

Editor's note: The caption for Plates 20 and 21 states that Gendje is
now called Elizabethpol. It has been renamed Kirovabad.

CONTENTS

ACKNOWLEDGMENTS

Special thanks to my parents and my daughter Karin for their constant support and encouragement.

Thanks to Randy Fleck for all his help and patience.

Thanks also to my friends Mort Gleberman and Duchess Strazzanti for their enthusiasm and their belief in me.

I particularly want to thank Chris Sheldon of Enchanted Yarns, Wallingford, Connecticut, for being so extraordinarily generous with her help and advice.

I'm grateful to Bob and Cris Read for allowing their lives to be disrupted by the use of their beautiful house for photography, and to Bill and Sandi Jensen for the use of their lovely store, WR & S Furniture in Cheyenne, Wyoming.

My sincere appreciation to Pat Gallagher and Kathy Heintzelman for their very helpful and valuable suggestions.

CREDITS

Interior arrangements by Cris Read; flower arrangements by Gilbert Goméz of Potpourri, Cheyenne, Wyoming; framing by Ernie Hastey of Cheyenne Framecraft, Cheyenne, Wyoming; hassock, Plate 4, designed and made by Rick LaVorgna; footstool, Plate 6, designed and made by Randy Fleck; bunching table, Plate 16, manufactured by James David.

INTRODUCTION

Rarely in the course of history has an art form been created with the enduring appeal of Oriental rugs. Throughout recorded time, their kaleidoscopic beauty and variety have been recognized as among the highest achievements in the decorative arts. The universal language of beauty expressed through motifs drawn from a cultural heritage of thousands of years (some motifs still in use are older than Babylon) is understood everywhere.

There are many reasons for the lasting charm of Oriental rugs. Most obvious is the innate beauty of decorative abstractions executed in rich and harmonious colors. Less obvious, but possibly more important, is the insight Oriental rugs can provide into the basic workings of the mind. Created by people who are often illiterate, whose simple lives are virtually devoid of stimulation beyond what a harsh environment provides, Oriental rugs are a tangible expression of the richness of mankind's inner vision. Perhaps, unencumbered by outer distractions, the mind's eye turns inward to the world of color, shape, and symbolism to which human imagination first awoke.

The completion of a single rug may require months or years. Only the sheer joy of self-expression can sustain such an effort; commercial considerations cannot. As the world in which Oriental rugs evolved is changing, the conditions that fostered intricacy and integrity of design are disappearing. It is a regrettable reality that rugs woven in the twentieth century seldom represent the concentration of artistic expression inherent in older pieces. Consequently, the demand for antique rugs has steadily risen, as has their cost, and these authentic works are increasingly unattainable. Few can hope to own a piece representing the finest traditions of craftsmanship, except through their own labors.

Needlepoint, I believe, is the best modern method of reproducing the richness and variety of Oriental rug designs. In its simplest form, needlepoint is ideal; the tight, flat surface of needlepoint fabric allows the patterns to show clearly, without the distraction of texture. The pieces designed for this book are not difficult to execute, but require only care, time, and a love of enduring beauty.

HISTORICAL BACKGROUND

No one knows just how ancient the art of weaving is, though it is known that the art was well developed in Egypt by the time of the pharaohs. Egyptian tomb paintings from 2000 B.C. show women weaving flax, and numerous examples of finely woven cloth have been discovered in excavated tombs. References to weaving also abound in the Bible. It is certain that by 3000 to 2000 B.C., weaving was an important art, practiced widely by craftsmen at various stages of cultural development, from primitive nomads to sophisticated city dwellers.

If little is known about the exact origin of weaving, even less is known about the early history of knotted rug weaving. Scholars and historians generally favor one of two opposing points of view. Some believe that the technique of weaving pile carpets is too complex to have arisen outside a city environment. The nomadic rug would, by this theory, be a poor imitation of the much finer city product. Others believe the knotting technique was developed by nomadic shepherds in an effort to simulate animal skins. Nomadic shepherds, unlike nomadic hunters, did not kill their animals for food or clothing, and consequently may have knotted bits of wool onto a coarse woven fabric in emulation of their hunting neighbors who used animal skins for protection against harsh climatic conditions. It is more believable that the sequence

of development was from nomads to villages and finally to city workshops, with the technique becoming increasingly refined in the process.

The nomads probably produced a rough and shaggy utilitarian rug of little aesthetic value for a considerable period of time before they developed designs and the clipping procedures necessary to show the designs to advantage. It is also possible that patterned rugs originated when the nomads came in contact with the decorative art of the cities. The geometric motifs common to nomadic rugs would therefore represent extremely simplified versions of much more elaborate designs, simplified because the primitive looms were frequently moved, and the nomads had to re-create the designs from memory. Some historians believe the traditional geometric motifs were inspired by the plant and animal forms of the stark nomadic environment. It is likely that the motifs were developed through a combination of both influences.

Although the early history of knotted rugs is subject to speculation because of the lack of surviving examples, stories of wonderful carpets abound in ancient literature. Homer mentions purple carpets in the *Iliad*, and numerous references are made by later Greek and Roman writers to the magnificent carpets and draperies of the East. Several early carpets became legendary, including the carpet of King Khosrau of Persia, which is reputed to have shown a garden complete with streams, paths, and trees. The branches and flowers were of precious stones, re-creating the beauty of spring for the king during the winter months. When the Persian Empire fell to Arab invaders in the seventh century, the carpet was cut up and shared by the conquerors. It is said that the original carpet was eighty-four feet square, woven entirely of silk.

Marco Polo praised the carpets of Asia Minor as the most beautiful in the world. Frequent references to carpets also appear in Arab and Persian literature between the eighth and fourteenth centuries, although it is not certain that these, or any other early references, are to knotted rugs. However, with the discovery in 1949 of a perfectly preserved knotted rug dating to 500 B.C., it becomes easier to believe that early writers were in fact referring to pile carpets. The Pazyryk Rug, as it is now known, was discovered in a royal burial mound excavated in the mountainous region of southern Siberia. The workmanship and design are of so high a quality that the rug must have been the product of a carpet-weaving art with a long history prior to 500 B.C. The rug may possibly have been woven by exceptionally skilled nomadic craftsmen, but the design elements as well as the dense knotting (225 knots per square inch) indicate that it may have originated in the Middle East, perhaps acquired by trade. Another rug fragment, dating to 700 B.C., was later found in the same area. This piece contains a remarkable 400 knots per square inch.

The next fragments found date from a full thousand years later. Several pieces were discovered in excavations along old caravan routes. In comparison with earlier finds, the workmanship of these fragments is coarse, containing only thirty or forty knots per square inch. In 1905, three large carpets and five fragments turned up in a mosque in Konya, Turkey, where they had been stored probably since the twelfth or thirteenth century. No pieces have yet been discovered for the intervening period.

By the fourteenth and fifteenth centuries, Europeans had begun importing substantial numbers of rugs from the East. The rugs were apparently highly valued. No examples survive, but pictorial evidence is ample, most notably in the works of Dutch and Italian masters. Venice had early become a center of trade with the East, and Venetian painters depicted Oriental carpets in religious, civil, and carnival activities. For special occasions, the Venetians hung rugs from windows, spread them on the streets, and even decorated their gondolas with carpets.

From the beginning of the sixteenth century, under court patronage, Persia and Anatolia produced great quantities of carpets that found their way all over the world. The quality of Persian rugs in particular reached a high point that has not been equaled since. The Safavid dynasty, Persia's first native rulers since the Arab conquest, had come into power at the end of the fifteenth century. With them came a classic period of artistic achievement that strongly influenced the art of rug weaving. Prior to this, Persian carpet weaving was probably no more than a village art. Small rugs with repetitive geometric designs often appear in the familiar Persian miniature paintings of the fifteenth century. However, under the Safavids, a curvilinear style developed—with flowing lines and flower patterns—influenced primarily by elaborate manuscript illuminations. Geometric figures could be woven from memory, but the more complex curvilinear designs required a cartoon prepared by an artist for the weaver to follow. It was this collaboration of book art and rug weaving that produced the golden age in rug design.

European rulers, who greatly prized the rich variety of Oriental rugs, acquired impressive collections. Large numbers of rugs appear in the household inventories of Charles V, Catherine de Medici, Mazarin, and Henry VIII. Eastern rulers often gave gifts of especially fine specimens to their European counterparts in the course of diplomatic negotiations.

The most famous example of rugs woven during the Safavid dynasty is the Ardebil Mosque Carpet, now in London's Victoria and Albert Museum. The rug, approximately 17½ x 34 feet, averages 350 knots per square inch, a total of more than 30 million knots. An inscription by the maker dates its completion to the year 1539. Many experts consider it the finest knotted rug in the world. Other rugs of similar quality from the same period can be seen in museums and palaces throughout the world.

The rug-weaving art remained lively until the end of the seventeenth century, when a general decline in production and quality set in. Continual political unrest prevailed throughout the eighteenth century. Most of the great royal courts of the world collapsed, and the elaborate creations of the Safavid dynasty were no longer in demand. Moreover, when the Safavid period itself was brought to an end by the Afghan invasion of 1736, the court looms were dismantled and rug weaving in Persia was left almost entirely in the hands of villagers and nomads.

Western interest in Oriental rugs revived by the middle of the nineteenth century, but by that time organized carpet making no longer existed in the Middle East. A completely new industry evolved to satisfy the sudden great demand from Europe and the United States; a dormant art was resurrected for strictly commercial reasons. Subsequently, merchants catering to the Western market attempted to control every aspect of the weaving process, from colors and designs to the size and shape of the rugs. Vast quantities of older carpets were also gathered by merchants in the towns and villages of the Middle East and sent to the West.

In 1891, more than four hundred pieces were exhibited in Vienna. The show was a huge success, stimulating the interest of collectors as well as scholars. Prior to this, very little had been known about the history and origin of Oriental rugs; in the seventeenth and eighteenth centuries all rugs from the East were referred to as Turkish, and in the nineteeth century they were all called Persian, regardless of style or origin. Almost overnight, the Western imagination was captured by the romance of camels and tents, palaces and mosques. Moreover, the artistic atmosphere of the period was dominated by the influence of the Impressionists, whose work led to a growing recognition of the power and vitality of abstract shapes and vivid colors. Form was suddenly more important than subject matter. The Oriental rug, particularly the nomadic rug, came to be appreciated as a work of art, a position it maintains today.

Production of commercial products, standardized to suit Western tastes, was at a peak in the early part of the twentieth century. By that time large segments of the Persian rug-weaving industry were in the control of American firms. When the Great Depression struck and Americans could no longer afford to purchase large numbers of carpets, the industry returned to Persian control and, consequently, to the higher standards of previous times. After World War II the Western market opened again, and Europeans took the lead in encouraging the return to traditional designs and workmanship. Americans and Europeans have maintained an active interest in Oriental rugs to the present day.

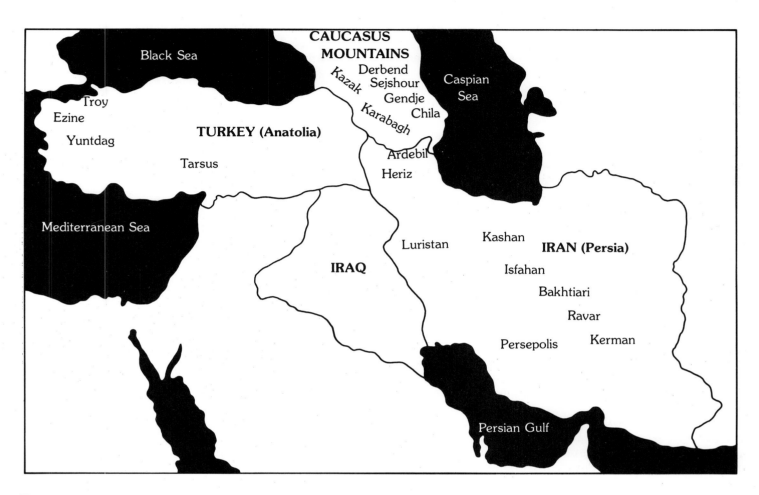

Persia

Persia, the fabled land of a *Thousand and One Nights,* has long been considered the world's greatest rug-weaving area. Since 1935, the land of the lion and the sun has been known as Iran, a name derived from the Middle Persian word for Aryan, the ancient racial stock to whom the Persians trace their ancestry. Rugs woven in this region are still referred to as Persian rugs.

The country is large (about two and a half times the size of Texas), but sparsely populated. Situated on a high plateau, Iran has an extreme climate; hot, dry summers alternate abruptly with bitter winters. The mountains that almost entirely encircle the plateau severely limit rainfall in the plains, although enough moisture falls to permit grazing over wide areas. Sheep are raised nearly everywhere, providing a ready supply of fine wool.

The continuous traditions of Persian rug weaving can be traced back 2,500 years to the Persian Empire. In its very early history, the area was contested by Medes, Assyrians, and Babylonians. In the middle of the sixth century B.C., scattered Persian tribes were united under the leadership of Cyrus, who created a powerful empire that included Babylonia, Syria, Palestine, Egypt, Cyprus, and the Greek islands.

Under Darius, the empire was extended as far as the Caucasus. The Greek historian Herodotus attributed the Persian Empire's astounding success not only to military genius, but also to the readiness with which the conquerors adopted foreign customs. The Persians considered themselves a civilizing force, which in fact they were; wars were conducted humanely, towns were spared, and religious tolerance prevailed. Persian art was enriched by assimilation of the best traditions from conquered cultures. Already the art of rug weaving was well developed; a carving dating to 500 B.C. at Persepolis, the capital, shows a Persian king receiving rugs as gifts.

A series of wars with Greece weakened the empire's influence sufficiently to force the Persians to abandon their civilizing mission. When Alexander the Great conquered the Persian Empire in 331 B.C., a period of cultural deterioration ensued. Persian traditions were not revived until the establishment of the Sassanian dynasty, which ruled from A.D. 224 to 651. Under the Sassanids, remnants of Greek influence disappeared, allowing a renaissance of native arts. Carpets of this period acquired a widespread and noteworthy reputation.

The Sassanids, although Persian in character, were intolerant of foreign religions. In the face of Roman Christianity's growing power, the Sassanids were forced to defend the Persian religion of Zoroaster. A struggle between Rome and Persia began, lasting nearly a hundred years, substantially weakening both powers. The religious matter was finally settled in the seventh century, when Arabs overthrew the Sassanids, supplanting both religions with Islam. In time, through intermarriage, the cultures merged to lay the foundation of language and custom, which was the beginning of modern Persia.

Mongols, who invaded Persia in the thirteenth century, destroyed cities and slaughtered most inhabitants, but not the craftsmen, who were put into the service of the conquerors. The incorporation of Chinese motifs into Persian rugs dates from this period. The destruction wrought by the Mongols fragmented Persia, opening the way for conquest by the Safavids in 1501. In spite of repeated skirmishes with the neighboring Turks, the Safavid dynasty ushered in an unparalleled period of artistic achievement. The famous Persian garden and hunting rugs made in court factories are considered the high point of rug-weaving art. The Safavid dynasty was brought to an end in 1736 after a series of Afghan invasions, which so weakened Persia that Russia and Turkey both seized large portions. The ancient boundaries were restored not long thereafter by a remarkable nomadic tribesman, Nadir Shah.

During the eighteenth century, Persia established contact with Europe through Britain and France. A period of increasing interaction with the West culminated in the rise of a constitutional movement early in the twentieth century. In 1926, the minister of war, Reza Khan Pahlavi, was crowned Shah of Persia. The new Shah built roads and railroads and established a postal service. The ancient nomadic way of life was suppressed, largely because the often fierce, always independent tribes presented a constant problem to modernizing the government. Shah Reza forced the nomads to settle in villages, sometimes at the cost of heavy loss of life to the flocks and subsequent disease and starvation to the people. His son, Mohammed Reza, adopted similar but less drastic policies, and many former nomads have been successfully resettled in villages.

Following the Afghan invasions in the early 1700s, court looms were dismantled, ending the organized carpet-weaving industry. It was not until the 1930s—when the Iranian Carpet Company was established to study and adapt the creations of the Safavid period for a growing Western market—that the industry began to recover.

During the last several decades, workshops have been set up by the government, and home weaving has been encouraged. As Iran's economy has become oil-based rather than craft-based, however, village weavers are often lured to city jobs by the promise of higher pay. Moreover, the government now requires compulsory education for children, thus removing from the rug-weaving industry a major source of cheap labor. As a result, expensive factory rugs catering to Western tastes have begun to outnumber authentic village and nomadic rugs.

Persia has been a land in which many ethnic groups have maintained independent traditions. Consequently, rug designs varying from starkly geometric to delicately floral can be found, although the elaborate curvilinear garden and hunting designs are considered most characteristically Persian. The vast majority of Persian weavers belong to the Shiite branch of the Moslem faith, a more liberal branch than the orthodox Sunni Moslems of Turkey. The prohibition of the Koran against depicting living creatures is not observed by the Persian rug weavers, as may be seen by the large number of mythological and real creatures that appear in their designs. Glowing pastel shades of blue, rose, and ivory are prevalent, particularly in newer rugs. Antique rugs are much brighter in color, often having a deep blue or red background.

Anatolia

Anatolia, meaning the Land of the Rising Sun, is the name applied to the part of Turkey that lies in Asia. Virtually no rugs are produced in the European section of Turkey; therefore the term "Anatolian rugs" refers generally to all rugs produced in Turkey.

Turkey possesses almost every type of topography and climate, from rich river valleys with stable, moderate weather to angular mountains with a harsh, inhospitable climate. A large central plateau consists primarily of rolling hills covered with vast grasslands. Sheep with strong, silky wool are raised all over the country; even in antiquity Anatolian sheep were famous for the quality of their wool.

Turkey is heir to centuries of rich and diverse cultural influences, each of which has contributed design elements that have gradually blended into a distinctively Anatolian style. Early in Turkey's history, Greeks settled the area, establishing colonies with such familiar and romantic names as Troy, Smyrna, and Pergamum. With the spread of the Persian Empire under Cyrus and Darius, the land was alternately in the possession of the Greeks and the Persians.

When Rome conquered the region, Christianity was initially planted more firmly in Anatolia than elsewhere, possibly due to the influence of Paul of Tarsus, a native Anatolian. The establishment of Constantinople as the capital of the Byzantine Empire began a period of Christian influence over the area that lasted nearly a thousand years. Then, in the eleventh century, vast migrations of Seljuk Turks arrived from the East, gradually supplanting Christianity with Islam. The Ottoman, or Turkish, Empire was established in 1300, beginning a long period of cultural and economic decline which lasted until the twentieth century. After World War I, the country adopted a Western orientation under the leadership of Ataturk. The opening of ports and the building of new roads revived Turkey as an active trade center.

Through centuries of changing rule, Greek and Armenian communities within Anatolia remained intact, maintaining their own religious and cultural traditions. During the time of the Turkish Empire, the Armenians, in spite of their Christian beliefs, had been a tolerated and prosperous merchant class. However, following the social revolution of World War I, severe political persecution drove hundreds of thousands of Greeks and Armenians out of Anatolia. Much of the carpet-weaving art went with them, leaving the rug industry severely crippled, a situation that persisted well into the twentieth century in spite of increased market demands from the West.

The government of Turkey has been instrumental in the current revival of Anatolian rug making. Factories and prison workshops have been established; the government also pro-

4

vides training, looms, and materials for home weavers. The technical quality of factory rugs is often quite high, though regrettably most of the originality of the spontaneous craft has been lost. A small but increasing number of village rugs are still made with traditional designs and methods. Many villagers have both the time and the patience required for the arduous task of rug weaving, and the sale of rugs often provides a source of additional income for people who are otherwise desperately poor. Nomadic weaving continues in Anatolia, although severely curtailed by the government's efforts to suppress and control the nomadic way of life. Tribes still range throughout the region, but the government maintains a close watch on migratory movements. No doubt the restrictions placed on personal freedom will cause a decline in the spontaneous originality of nomadic designs, which in the past have reflected the independence of tribal existence.

Anatolian rugs are characteristically rectilinear in style, only rarely including the floral elements so common in Persian rugs. The Koran forbids the depiction of living creatures, a prohibition that has encouraged the devout Sunni Moslems to develop geometric patterns, although today the restriction is not observed as scrupulously as in the past. The largest number of prayer rugs has always come from Anatolia, where the custom of turning to Mecca five times a day for prayer still prevails. Green, the prophet's sacred color, was once seen exclusively in prayer rugs, but, with the relaxation of many old customs, the use of green has become more widespread. In general, Anatolian weavers favor bright colors, rather than the pastel shades frequently preferred by Persians.

The Caucasus

The Caucasus Mountains, stretching between the Black Sea and the Caspian, form a natural barrier between Europe and Asia. At the end of the eighteenth century, a German anthropologist, who erroneously believed the Caucasus to be the original home of Indo-Europeans, popularized the name by designating the white race Caucasians.

The mountains are divided into two groups, the Greater Caucasus and the Lesser Caucasus. The Greater Caucasus, bordering the Russian steppes, consist of a range with elevations varying from 9,000 to 18,000 feet, forming a barrier 60 to 100 miles wide. To the south, the more densely inhabited Lesser Caucasus border the Anatolian Plateau and the mountains of northern Iran. The climate is often savage; hot, dry summers are replaced by winters that bring constant snow, wind, and subzero temperatures. The sheep, which through generations have been bred to survive the inhospitable conditions of the mountains, produce a tough, springy wool.

For centuries, the Caucasus have served as a corridor for countless migrations of refugees fleeing from persecution. The Romans established colonies in the Caucasus, later to be dominated by the Byzantine Empire. A period of Arab rule was followed by Mongol invasions. In recent history, the Caucasus have been contested by Turks and Persians. Not until the Russians subjugated the Tartars were the boundaries settled, with the czarist regime claiming the area from the Persians.

Following the upheavals of the Russian Revolution, widespread social and economic changes were instituted by the Soviets. The traditional crafts were largely abandoned as mining and other new industries employed increasing numbers of village inhabitants. After World War II, the Russians nationalized the rug-weaving industry, establishing factories and standardizing materials and designs. The rugs produced under these conditions tend to lack distinction of any kind.

Rugs woven in the Caucasus before the Russian Revolution can be identified by their bold geometric patterns and robust colors. Because the refugees who settled in the mountains were often fiercely independent nomads or seminomads unwilling to be subjugated by their conquerors, historical fluctuations have had much less influence on the design of Caucasian rugs than might be expected. Traditionally, special motifs and patterns have been associated with every tribe and village. Intermarriage and social exchange have gradually blurred the distinctions, but a unique Caucasian style has nevertheless persisted. Flowers, animals, and common objects are frequently stylized into almost unrecognizable angular designs. Red, blue, yellow, green, and ivory are by far the most predominant colors, as they are readily obtained from natural sources. Caucasian rugs are usually small; the limitations of primitive living conditions have made the production of large pieces impractical. The unpredictable irregularity of spontaneous folk craft has always been considered one of the major charms of Caucasian rugs.

DESIGN ELEMENTS

One of the great fascinations of Oriental rugs is that the most amazing variety of designs has developed within rather rigid limitations. Virtually all Oriental rugs follow the same basic layout: a large central area called the field, and a main border surrounded on either side by one or more secondary borders. This framework could have developed any number of other ways. For example, there might have been borders at only two ends of the rug, or there might have been a much less rigid border structure, or there might have been no border at all. Yet, within this almost unvarying basic structure, the rug weavers have created a rich, exciting array of colors and patterns.

In attempting to classify the various patterns, it may be helpful to separate them into five basic styles:
1. The prayer rug with an arch, or *mihrab,* at one end.
2. The repeat pattern, in which a single motif is repeated throughout the field.
3. The all-over design, in which related, but not repeating, patterns cover the entire field.
4. Compartmentalized patterns with the same or differing designs enclosed in a grid or block.
5. Medallion designs, generally containing a center medallion with a quartered medallion in the four corners.

In general, rugs with graceful curvilinear designs of interlacing flowers are woven in cities by people of education and sophisticated artistic sensibilities. Intricate flower designs are most prevalent in Persian rugs, especially those woven in the great cities such as Isfahan, Tabriz, and Kerman. The complexity of the designs requires that complete patterns be prepared for the weavers. Only in the cities do the resources for such efforts exist. Rectilinear rugs of all-over or repeating designs are, for the most part, produced by village weavers who have the time and stability to undertake tasks requiring considerable attention, but not the artistic sophistication required for curvilinear designs. Moreover, rectilinear designs can more readily be woven from memory. Strictly geometric designs are usually the product of nomads, whose stark existence is reflected in the bold patterns they weave.

Symbolism

A great deal has been written about the element of symbolism in Oriental rugs. Some scholars are adamant in insisting that secret meanings have been assigned entirely by romantic Westerners. Others are certain that every little group of knots is heir to centuries of deep and mysterious symbolic associations. As with so many other issues, the truth probably lies somewhere in between. Undoubtedly, Westerners have sometimes superimposed meaning where none existed, but just as certainly the weavers must have included motifs of special importance and meaning to them. Considering the astounding number of myths and fairy tales, talismans and charms, ceremonies and rituals human beings have created, it would be hard to believe that a race of essentially poetic and superstitious people could have refrained from weaving messages and meanings into their rugs.

Probably modern weavers who produce rugs for commercial reasons use ancient symbols purely for their effect, but a village weaver or nomad who weaves a rug for personal use would be likely to choose motifs as much for their traditional meaning as for their decorative quality.

In any case, various motifs are generally believed to have specific symbolic meaning. Trees and flowers hold special significance for the Oriental rug weaver. The idea of immortality is represented by the Tree of Life motif—a stylized tree, often shortened to look more like a spray of flowers anchored in a small vase. The cypress tree is also used to represent life after death and serves as a sign of mourning as well. The weeping willow, with its gracefully drooping branches seeking the ground, is a reminder of death. Both the pomegranate and ears of grain mean fertility and, by association, prosperity. The pomegranate also denotes happiness and fulfillment, understandable since its moisture is particularly appreciated by desert people.

Lost in antiquity is the significance of one of the most frequently used designs, a pear-shaped figure with a little hooked piece extending from the narrow end, called a *boteh.* A fanciful interpretation suggests it bears the shape of a closed fist that has been dipped in blood and pressed on paper, an ancient method of sealing documents. An equally colorful story claims the shape is that of the Indus River looping toward the plains of upper Kashmir. Still a third interpretation has the *boteh* derived from the shape of the great diamond in the crown of Persia.

The rose, usually in highly simplified form, also appears frequently. Its presence is a reminder of an old Persian belief that life, like a rose, is beautiful in spite of its thorns. Another predominant design, generally a diamond shape with a series of hooked protrusions all around, is suggestive of a tarantula, and is intended as a charm to dispel fear of this creature.

While there may be a dispute about the validity of assigning symbolic importance to various motifs, there is general agreement that colors do in fact convey specific meaning. Red, the most frequently used color, denotes happiness, joy, life, and all that is good and virtuous. Blue is the color of solitude and truth, while orange represents piety or sorrow. To Moslems, green is the sacred color of the prophet's coat, and hence of paradise, life, and immortality. As such, it is rarely used by devout Moslem weavers, although it may occasionally be seen on prayer rugs. Non-Islamic weavers use green freely. The idea of power is represented by gold and yellow because of its obvious association with the glitter of wealth. Purple, in the East as elsewhere, is the imperial color, the color of royalty. Rose and pink reflect divine wisdom. The earth color, brown, signifies fertility. Black is rarely found because of its association with evil and destruction; by a curious coincidence, the traditional method of dyeing wool black corrodes the yarn so badly that black areas on rugs are always the first to wear down. In the East, white rather than black is the universal color of mourning, death, and, subsequently, of peace.

Prayer Rug

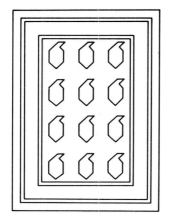

Repeat Pattern

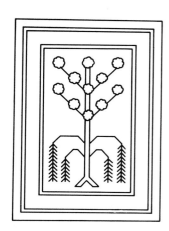

All-over Design

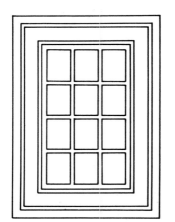

Compartmentalized Pattern

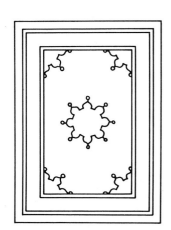

Medallion Design

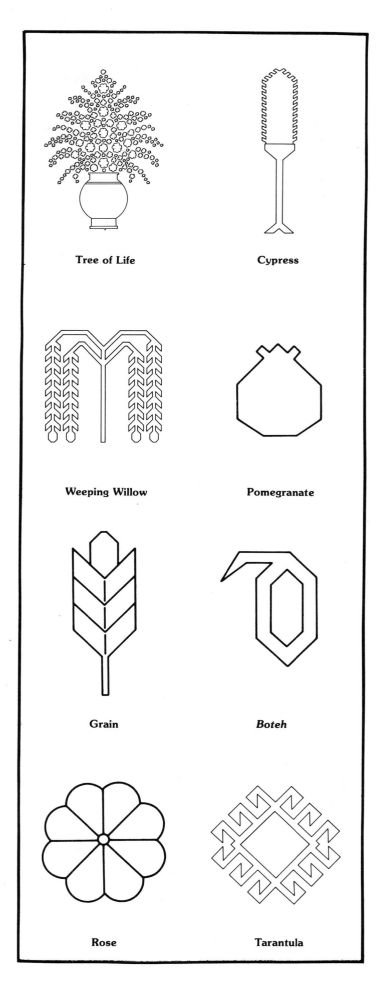

Tree of Life

Cypress

Weeping Willow

Pomegranate

Grain

Boteh

Rose

Tarantula

REPEAT MOTIFS

On the original rugs from which these designs were derived, a single motif would be larger than is practical for needlepoint. An individual flower might be several inches in width, requiring as many as a hundred or more knots from one side to the other. Moreover, most Oriental rug motifs (except stark nomadic designs) are somewhat irregular in shape, which can make it difficult to follow the pattern.

To make it easier to work from a graph, and still convey the visual impression of the original designs, I have simplified the most common rug motifs into a series of small geometric units. These units, which appear singly and in multiple variations, are the basis of every design in this book. An individual piece may be curvilinear or angular, yet the essential design elements are always the same.

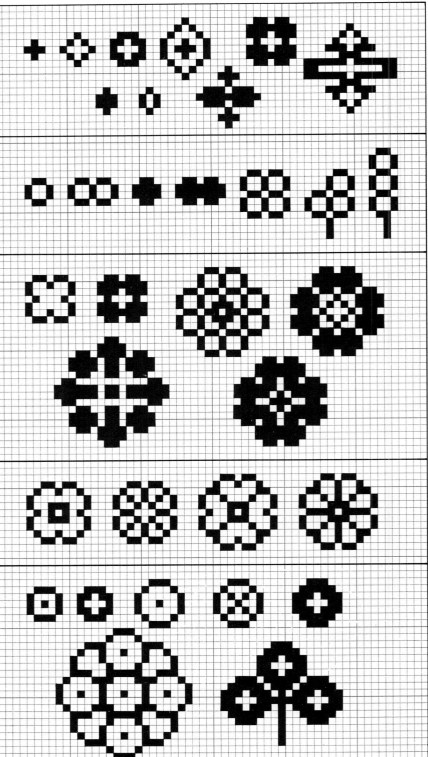

The simplest motif is a cross of three stitches each way. It appears alone or as the center of a larger motif. Sometimes it is elongated by the addition of two or three extra rows of stitches in the center.

A simple square of four stitches with an extension of two stitches on each side forms one of the most frequently used motifs. It may be seen either solidly filled or with a separate color in the center.

The same shape may be joined in numerous other ways, a stitch or two being omitted or added in order to allow a decorative center.

Expanding the basic shape by the addition of one or two diagonal stitches allows the formation of several simple and useful flower motifs.

Other small flower designs are formed when the square of four stitches is enlarged to nine stitches, with an extension of three stitches on each side. The addition of a diagonal stitch forms a common variation, which appears most often alone, though sometimes in a group.

Each group of motifs begins with a single basic shape, which becomes more elaborate as it is combined with other basic shapes or expanded by the addition of one or more diagonal stitches. Three shapes—a cross, a square, and a stepladder—are the basis of the entire sequence. The final patterns may seem complex but are in fact easy to stitch, due to the simplicity and repetition of the motifs.

Familiarizing yourself with these small geometric units will enable you to work areas of repeating pattern without constant reference to the graphs. Flower and border designs that initially appear ornate will be seen to be derived from the original units, the shapes of which can be memorized easily. Often, you will find it unnecessary to count stitches if you recognize the structure of the motifs.

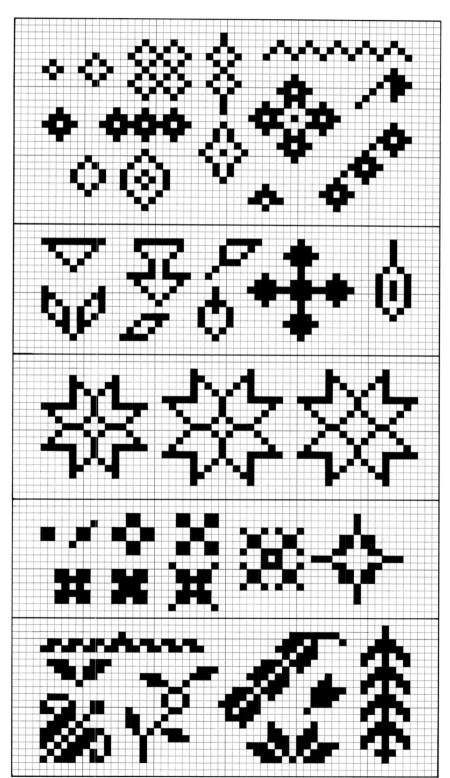

A stepladder design of diagonal stitches is often seen alone or in combinations, both in the field pattern and the smaller geometric designs of the minor borders.

Together with a series of straight lines, the stepladder is used to form many other shapes.

An eight-pointed star appears in several sizes and variations, but is always formed from a simple combination of diagonal stitches joining straight lines.

A square of four stitches is the basis of several decorative designs, which occasionally are embellished by a few extra stitches.

Configurations of two or three staggered stitches may be seen in simple borders, or as leaves and buds in combination with flowers and stems.

THE
DESIGNS

Plate 1. Laver Kerman

LAVER KERMAN

Plate 2. Laver Kerman, Persia. The village of Ravar, known incorrectly in the West as Laver, is reputed to produce particularly fine Kerman-pattern rugs, often in a prayer design. The largest number of prayer rugs comes from Turkey, where the devout Sunni Moslems turn toward Mecca five times a day. The somewhat less strict Shiite Moslems of Persia produce a smaller number of prayer rugs, which are valued greatly for their decorative quality. The pointed arch, called a *mihrab,* is derived from mosque architecture. The center of the arch supports a hanging mosque lamp. The mass of flowers spreading from a small vase represents a simplified version of the Tree of Life design, symbolizing immortality. Two Pillars of Wisdom support the arch. Originally these may have represented the pillars at the temple of Persepolis, the capital of the Persian Empire.

HERIZ

Plates 3 and 4. Heriz, Persia. Heriz is the largest of a group of villages producing rugs of similar design. A large central medallion is characteristic, as is the use of pink and red color schemes. In this piece, the innermost medallion contains tulips, while the outer medallion is decorated by cypresses signifying life after death, and ears of grain signifying prosperity. Numerous roses adorn the field, attesting to the Persian belief that life, like a rose, is beautiful in spite of the thorns. The border consists primarily of stylized carnations.

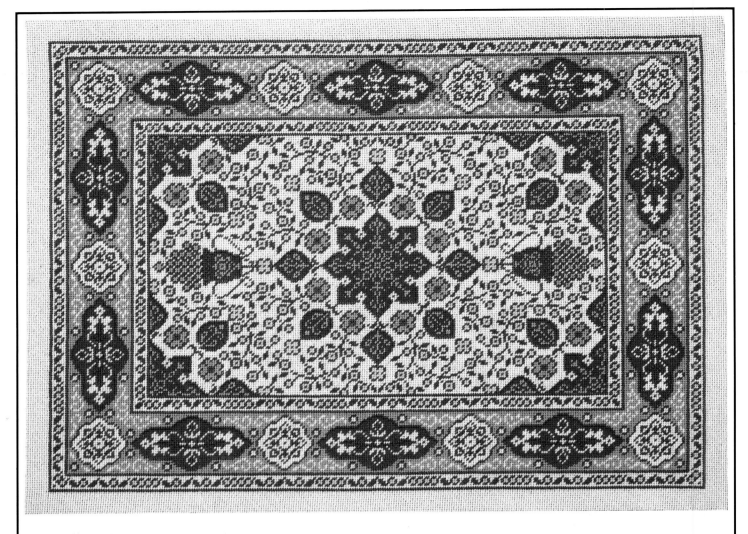

KASHAN

Plates 5 and 6. Kashan, Persia. This harmonious piece owes its design to one of the world's most famous rugs— the Ardebil Mosque Carpet, which is displayed at the Victoria and Albert Museum in London. The original, completed in 1539, is 17½ x 34 feet, with about 350 knots per square inch. Many experts consider it the finest knotted carpet in the world. The original color scheme of gold, rust, and green on dark blue has been replaced here by the delicate pastels used in modern Persian adaptations. The Ardebil Mosque Carpet derives its name from the fact that it was discovered in a mosque in the town of Ardebil. It is believed the carpet was actually woven in Kashan, one of Persia's finest weaving centers. An ancient legend suggests it was from Kashan that the journey of the Three Wise Men originated.

TREE & GARDEN

Plates 7 and 8. Tree and Garden Carpet, Persia. Under the reign of Shah Abbas in the sixteenth century, a number of elaborate carpets were woven with designs representing formal court gardens. Only four or five pieces have been preserved, one of which was acquired by the Metropolitan Museum of Art in New York from the famous collection of Joseph V. McMullan. It is not known precisely where the rug was woven, though it is believed that it may have been at a workshop in northern Persia, rather than at the court factory in Isfahan.

LURISTAN

Plates 9 and 10. Luristan, Persia. Luristan rugs are woven by the Lur tribe, which still partly follows the traditional nomadic way of life. As is frequently the case with nomadic rugs, this lively design is full of symbols that have special meaning to people whose lives are often harsh and difficult. Interestingly, the willow, which symbolizes sorrow and death, is joined to a cypress tree, symbolic of life after death. The small bird on top of the tree represents a peacock, the sacred bird. The birds in the border are probably meant to be doves, birds of peace.

YUNTDAG

Plates 11 and 12. Yuntdag, Anatolia. The village of Yuntdag is located at the base of a mountain (*dag* means mountain in Turkish) close to Bergama, one of western Anatolia's major rug centers. Though undoubtedly influenced by the designs of Bergama, the Yuntdag weavers produce rugs that are unique in color and style. The combination of mauve, green, and brick red is characteristic only of Yuntdag carpets. Moslems, who are sensitive to the symbolic value of color, are partial to prayer rugs woven in Yuntdag. Green, the prophet's sacred color, is seldom used by Moslem weavers except in prayer rugs, such as the one from which this design was derived. The lavender square in the center would be the part of the rug on which the worshiper kneels. Because few rugs from the village of Yuntdag ever reach commercial centers, their unusual style is not generally familiar to Western eyes.

KAZAK

Plates 13 and 14. Kazak, Caucasus. Kazak rugs perfectly exemplify the nomadic rug. Bold colors, especially the warm red obtained from the madder plant, are combined with equally bold geometric designs. The main border, called zigzag, is commonly found on rugs from this area, though its exact design can vary considerably. The blue shapes with hooked protrusions, often called latch hooks, that surround the central medallions, have their origin in a tarantula design that nomads wove into their rugs to help dispel the fear of these creatures. Kazak rugs are named for a style and general area rather than a tribe or town. In the past, however, books have romanticized the term by declaring it to be derived from "cossack."

EZINE

Plates 15 and 16. Ezine, Anatolia. The village of Ezine lies near Canakkale, close to the ruins of Troy. It was in Canakkale and its surrounding villages that the Anatolian rugs so frequently seen in late Renaissance paintings were woven. Holbein rugs, named for the painter who made them famous, are the direct ancestors of patterns such as this one. The starlike medallion is characteristic of rugs from Ezine. The scroll border probably originates in elaborate Kufic script figures that have been increasingly simplified over the centuries.

BAKHTIARI

Plate 18. Bakhtiari, Persia. The Bakhtiaris are one of the largest and most powerful tribes of Persia. A few are still nomadic, but most are now settled in numerous farm villages. They have long been among the most prosperous tribes; in fact, Bakhtiari means "the lucky ones" in Persian. The rugs bearing the Bakhtiari name are not woven exclusively by that tribe. Many are the products of Turkish weavers living in villages surrounding the Bakhtiari area. The design frequently is enclosed in a series of squares, each of which contains a garden motif of symbolic importance. The Tree of Life, seen here in the form of a vase and flowers, is common, as is the willow, symbol of death and mourning. Green, blue, and ivory are more predominant in Bakhtiari rugs than the red so prevalent in most Persian rugs.

SEJSHOUR

Plate 19. Sejshour, Caucasus. Sejshour, a village near the town of Kuba, is known for its use of a strong diagonal cross motif, usually attached to a stylized flower medallion. Carpets bearing this design are often called Georgian rugs on the possibly erroneous supposition that the crossed beams represent the Georgian cross. Sejshour weavers are fond of the unusual rosy peach color in the inner border. The outer border, called Running Dog, almost always appears in blue and white.

GENDJE

Plates 20 and 21. Gendje, Caucasus. The town of Gendje, now called Elizabethpol, has long been a trade center, located about halfway between the Black Sea and the Caspian. Its position as a stopping place for caravans made it a collecting point for carpets woven in the surrounding areas. Gendje weavers typically favor a field of diagonal stripes filled with small geometric motifs (Plate 21). The use of light blue and white is more prevalent in rugs from Gendje than in any other rugs woven in the Caucasus. Star and flower shapes are also common, though the bold treatment they receive in the top piece (Plate 20) is rather unusual. The design seems to have been inspired by the formal garden carpets of the sixteenth century. The simplification of complex designs by unsophisticated weavers is charmingly evident here.

DERBEND

Plate 22. Derbend, Caucasus. Derbend, located by the Caspian Sea on the major crossroad between Persia and Russia, produces rugs of typically Caucasian geometric design. The use of shades of blue, especially dark blue, is particularly characteristic of rugs woven here. It is also common to find stylized human figures in white, as may be seen in the border. The protrusions emanating from the center medallion are probably derived from a pattern frequently found in Caucasian rugs, called the Ram's Horn. The red shapes at the inner corner of the border represent pomegranates, the symbol of happiness and fulfillment, undoubtedly because their moisture is highly prized by the nomads.

KARABAGH

Plate 23. Karabagh, Caucasus. Karabagh, an area in the southern Caucasus, is known best for this design, generally called a Sunburst. At one time it was termed an Eagle Kazak, possibly because it was believed that the elaborate center medallion represented the eagle on the Russian coat of arms. However, the origin of the design can actually be traced to a much earlier style known as Dragon rugs, in which twisting stylized dragon shapes emanated from a floral center medallion. Over the centuries, the dragon has disappeared, but the Karabagh weavers have retained the floral nature of the center medallion, surrounding it with a border commonly found on Caucasian rugs. The eight-pointed border star, or Star of Solomon, was originally a Jewish symbol that was adopted by Islam and renamed the Jewel of Mohammed. Legend states that King Solomon wore a ring with an eight-pointed star that had oracular powers.

CHILA

Plate 24. Chila, Caucasus. Chila rugs are known mainly for patterns such as this one, called the *Boteh-Chila*, which typically consist of a blue field covered with large decorated cone-shaped figures. The *boteh* is one of the most frequently used motifs in Oriental rugs, though its precise significance is now obscure. A fanciful interpretation suggests it bears the shape of a closed fist that has been dipped in blood and pressed on paper, an ancient method of sealing documents. Some claim the *boteh* derives its shape from a loop in the Indus River as it turns toward the plains of Kashmir. A third interpretation suggests the *boteh* emulates the shape of the great diamond in the crown of Persia. Blue, in all its shades, is a great favorite with Chila weavers, and is usually the predominant color.

MATERIALS

The process of making a piece of needlepoint can be enjoyed as much as the finished piece. The pleasure of watching patterns grow and colors begin to interplay can be just as great as the pleasure of seeing your finished piece in its proper setting. Using the right tools and handling quality materials are aesthetic experiences in themselves. There are always shortcuts and there are always inferior materials, but considering the amount of time you will invest in your work, it seems pointless not to use methods and materials that make the work as pleasant, and the final result as lasting, as possible.

Canvas

Needlepoint is worked on a canvas that looks very much like a coarse window screen. The threads are generally cotton, though linen is also used. Cotton is the most readily available and provides a strong, smooth working surface. Linen canvases are usually of a high quality, but are more expensive than cotton.

Canvas is stiffened with a starch, or sizing. The sizing helps to preserve the shape of the canvas and keeps the threads in place, so that the spaces, and thus the stitches, will be all the same size. When the finished piece is dampened, the sizing dissolves, leaving the work soft and pliable.

Two types of canvas weave, penelope and mono, are available. Penelope canvas is a double mesh, and mono, as the name implies, a single mesh. This means that the intersection of horizontal and vertical threads consists of four strands in a penelope canvas and two strands in a mono canvas. Penelope is preferable for work that requires intricate details because both large (gros point) and small (petit point) stitches can be worked on the same canvas.

On mono canvas, the stitch size is uniform throughout. All the designs in this book were worked on mono canvas since the stitch size never varies on the same piece. Also, because the spaces on a mono canvas are larger than on a penelope, the mono is easier on the eyes.

Mono canvas comes in both white and unbleached. The unbleached is said to remain crisp longer than the white. I prefer the white because the designs, which are most often stitched in vivid colors, look better while being worked on a white background; once the piece is finished, however, this becomes irrelevant.

The gauge of the canvas is also important, because the finished size of the piece, as well as its character, depends on the number of stitches per inch. Many sizes, from very coarse to very fine, are available, but the only sizes used in this book are ten to the inch and twelve to the inch. Size 10 canvas, with 100 stitches per square inch, is used for nomadic designs because the diagonal stitches show clearly and reflect the strong geometric quality of the original pieces. Size 12 canvas, with 144 stitches per square inch, is used for the more delicate curvilinear designs. The proper canvas gauge is given with the instructions for each piece.

The working size of the canvas is also given. This includes a three-inch border of unworked canvas on each side, which is used for pulling the finished piece into shape for blocking, and which provides an edge for stapling the piece to a blocking board.

Before purchasing a canvas, check the entire piece for flaws. There should be no knotted, weak, or uneven threads. The squares should be uniform in size, and the entire canvas should have a smooth, glossy appearance, indicating that the threads are coated evenly with sizing. Stretching the finished piece places a considerable strain on the threads, and it would be unfortunate to have an imperfect thread break in the process.

Yarn

The wool used in needlepoint must be soft and pliable, yet have the strength to withstand the abrasive effect of being pushed and pulled through the canvas numerous times. Persian wool is the finest and most versatile yarn available. Every piece in this book has been worked with Persian wool from Paternayan Brothers, whose yarns are widely available in a wonderful variety of colors. The exact shade of each color used is listed by number with the instructions for each piece. Since Paternayan makes several hundred shades, it would be wise to work with the given colors. A change in the value of any color affects all the other colors and can easily destroy the harmony of the finished work.

Paternayan Persian yarn can be purchased by either the skein or the strand. The number of strands of each color I used in each piece is listed with its color number. However, because every person stitches with a slightly different tension, and uses yarn with a varying degree of efficiency, the total amount required can differ by several strands. Purchase a few extra strands of every color, especially if the supplier isn't right around the corner. Yarn for patterned areas can be purchased a bit at a time because slight variations in shade won't show, but yarn for solid background areas should be purchased at the same time and from the same skein so there can be no possibility of a difference in dye lots.

When a whole skein is purchased, it should be untwisted, and one cut should be made through the entire thickness. This gives you about ninety-five strands, each of which is about sixty-six inches long. The strand count given in the instructions is based on this length. When you have counted out the proper number, cut the strands in half to make a more convenient working length.

Persian yarn is a three-ply wool. Each strand consists of three threads that are lightly twisted together. All three threads are used on a 10-mesh canvas, but only two are used on a 12 mesh. To separate the threads, pull one of the three away from the others with one hand, while holding the remaining two threads with the other hand. Pull the single strand away gently, allowing the yarn to untwist itself as you separate it.

If Paternayan Persian yarn is not available at your local store, write to Paternayan Brothers, 312 East 95th Street, New York, NY 10028, for the name of the store nearest you that carries their full line of products. In Britain, write to Needle Art House, Ltd., Wakefield, England WF2 9SG.

Needles

Needlepoint needles, also called tapestry needles, are short and blunt, with a long eye. (The blunt point prevents splitting the threads of the canvas as the needle is pushed through, and the long eye facilitates threading with wool.) They come in sizes varying from number 26 (the smallest) to number 13 (the largest). The needle should be a size that allows it to pass through the spaces of the canvas without distorting them. I use a number 20 needle for both the 10- and the 12-mesh canvas. However, the slightly larger number 18 needle can also be used on the 10-mesh canvas. The advantage is that the larger eye is easier to thread with the thicker yarn used in working on 10-mesh canvas, and the disadvantage is that it doesn't slide through the spaces as smoothly as the smaller needle. Try them both and use whichever size is more comfortable.

Good tapestry needles are made of steel, which gradually oxidizes from the moisture in the air and on your hands. This causes the needle to lose its smoothness and offer resistance, which slows down your work. Purchase a pincushion with an emery or sand bag attached to it. Passing the needle through the bag several times will polish it and prevent the needle from dragging.

It's a good idea to keep several needles on hand. You will often have lengths of leftover yarn that can be used later. It saves wear and tear on the yarn if you don't have to pull it from the needle, only to rethread it again at another time.

Scissors

Invest in a good pair of small embroidery scissors with sharp, pointed blades. The tip of the blade should pass easily under an individual stitch, so mistakes can be cut out.

Thimble

A thimble is a very useful item for working on needlepoint. Pushing a needle through a canvas countless times can be hard on the fingers, and a thimble prevents blisters and sore spots from forming. A Band-Aid can also be wrapped around the finger to cushion it, but a thimble is really a much more elegant solution. At first it may seem awkward to use one, but the benefits are well worth the effort.

A silver thimble is best; gold is too soft, and porcelain is too heavy. Buy the kind that has a glass top with small round indentations in it. The pressure required to push a relatively large needle and a long strand of heavy yarn through a canvas is enough to eventually poke a hole through the thimble if the tip is silver. A glass top lasts indefinitely.

PREPARING THE CANVAS

Binding

Before working on the canvas, bind the edges with masking tape or seam binding so the canvas doesn't ravel, and the yarn won't snag on the rough edges as you work. Masking tape can be folded over the edges quickly and easily, and it works well enough during the stitching. However, I find that when I wet the finished work prior to stretching it, the water loosens the tape, causing it to fall off when the piece is pulled into shape. Using a sewing machine to stitch seam binding on the edges requires more effort, but it holds far better during the blocking process, and is much more attractive to work with.

Center Stitch

The easiest way to find the center stitch is to fold the canvas in half each way, creasing the center line slightly with your fingers each time. The intersection of the two creases will be your center stitch. Use this as the starting point in working from the graphs.

Mark the center stitch on your canvas, either with a felt-tip pen or a strand of yarn. If you use a pen, choose a light color and be sure the ink is indelible or it may bleed onto your needlepoint when you wet the finished canvas. If you use yarn for marking, pass a piece through the center stitch and make a loose knot above and below the canvas so the yarn won't slip through.

Frame

Needlepoint may be worked either on your lap or on a frame. The greatest advantage of working with the piece on your lap is that each stitch can be made with one motion. The needle can be brought in and out of the canvas at the same time. With the work attached to a frame, each stitch requires two motions. One hand is held above the canvas and pushes the needle through, while the other hand is held beneath the canvas and pulls the needle down. Before the next stitch, the hand under the canvas pokes the needle through to the top, and the hand above the canvas pulls it out. It sounds like more work, but I find this method faster. When I hold the work on my lap, I have to make an extra movement in order to position the yarn properly for the next stitch. Also, when the strand is long, it twists easily, often forming an annoying knot just as the yarn is being pulled through.

The greatest advantage of working on a frame is that the work stays crisp and clean, and the stitches are more even. The sizing remains intact longer than when the piece receives constant handling. Stitching is easier because the threads of the canvas are held in place, and the spaces remain uniform in size. When I work a piece on my lap the moisture from my hands dissolves some of the sizing, allowing the threads to shift and causing the spaces to become uneven in size.

The stitch used throughout this book distorts the canvas diagonally. Blocking straightens the canvas, but the less distorted it is, the easier the blocking process will be. A piece that has been worked on a frame will be less distorted than one that has not.

All things considered, I strongly recommend working on a frame. Invest in a standing floor frame that is sturdy and well made. Table models are available, but a floor frame is more comfortable to work at, and gives you the added pleasure of enjoying your growing work as a decorative item in the room.

Narrower sizes are made, but a thirty-six-inch scroll frame will accommodate larger pieces comfortably, and small pieces can be worked on it just as easily.

The canvas should be stitched to the cloth tape on the wooden dowels with a sewing machine, or by hand with a running stitch. Position the canvas on the underside of the tape, so that when the canvas is rolled up, its edge will be held between the tape and the dowel. Make sure the canvas is centered evenly across both dowels or it will twist when you roll it up.

Don't be discouraged by the initial awkwardness of working on a frame. The difficulty of guiding the needle to the proper space with the hand under the canvas is soon overcome, though it may take several attempts at first.

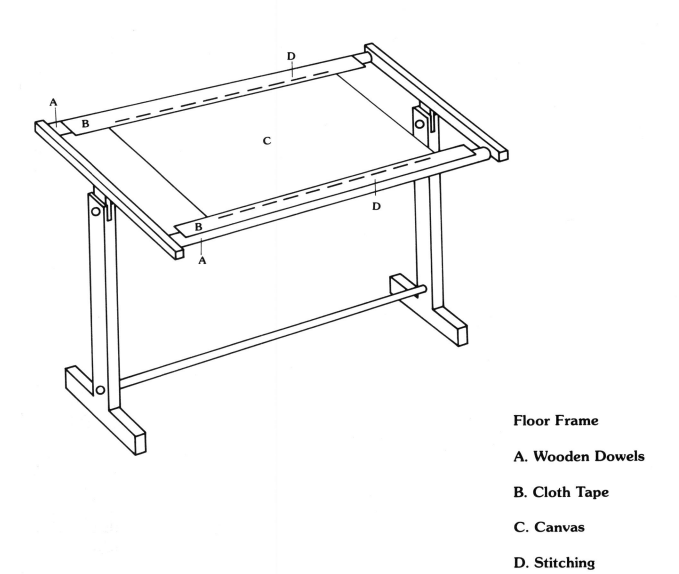

Floor Frame

A. Wooden Dowels

B. Cloth Tape

C. Canvas

D. Stitching

THE STITCH

Oriental designs depend on harmony of pattern and color for their beauty. Texture would be an unnecessary and unwanted distraction. For this reason, only the simplest needlepoint stitch is used in these pieces.

The basic stitch may be worked in either of two ways, but its appearance on the front of the work is always the same: the stitch slants from lower left to upper right, and covers one intersection of the horizontal and vertical threads of the canvas. The two names given the stitch, the continental and the basket weave, refer to the sequence in which the stitches are made. The continental consists primarily of placing stitches side by side or end to end. The basket weave consists of a more intricate pattern of dovetailing stitches along the slanted side of a triangle shape.

The continental stitch is used only for outlines and details. It is the easier stitch to learn, but should never be relied upon to cover large areas. Because the direction of the yarn on both the front and back of the work is slanted, the continental stitch exerts a strong diagonal pull on the canvas, severely distorting it.

The basket-weave stitch is essential for covering large areas. The interwoven pattern of alternating horizontal and vertical threads that this stitch forms on the back of the canvas exerts an equal pull in each direction. This prevents any serious distortion of the canvas.

Practice the stitches first on a piece of scrap canvas held on your lap, working each stitch in one motion as shown in the drawings. When you're ready to work on canvas that is attached to a frame, remember that the stitches will be made in exactly the same sequence and direction, but will require two motions, with one hand held below the canvas and the other above it.

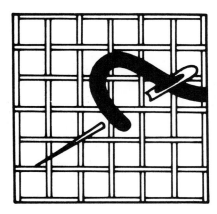

First Stitch

1. Bring your needle up through a space, working from the back of the canvas to the front. Poke the needle down through the space one row above and one mesh to the right. Bring the needle to the front again through the space just to the left of your starting point.

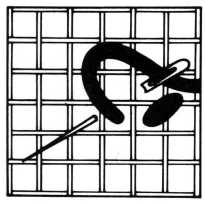

Second Stitch

2. For the second stitch, poke the needle down again through the space one row above and one mesh to the right, bringing it out to the left of the second stitch. The needle is plied diagonally.

Vertical Rows

3. To work a vertical row, bring the needle out below the starting point of each preceding stitch.

The Continental Stitch

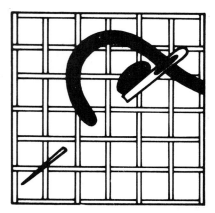

Diagonal Line, Right to Left

4. To work a diagonal line from right to left, start with a continental stitch, and bring your needle up through the hole one row below and one mesh to the left of your starting point. Bring the needle back down in the space where the first stitch started. The needle is plied diagonally.

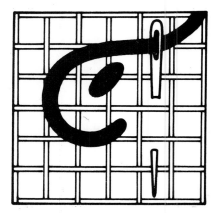

Diagonal Line, Left to Right

5. To work a diagonal line in the opposite direction, make a continental stitch, and bring the needle to the front of the canvas through the second space below the exit point of the last stitch.

The Basket-Weave Stitch

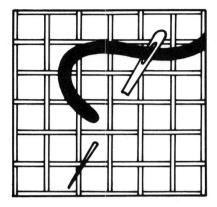

First Stitch

1. Starting at upper right, make one continental stitch, bringing the needle out in the space just below the first stitch.

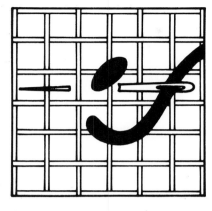

Second Stitch

2. Insert the needle in the space immediately to the right of the first stitch, passing it behind the stitch, and bringing it out in the space immediately to the left of the first stitch.

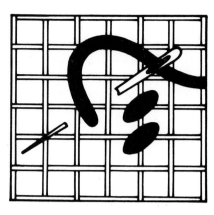

Third Stitch

3. Complete the stitch on the left of the first stitch, bringing the needle out in the space to the left of the third stitch. You are now beginning to form the triangle shape.

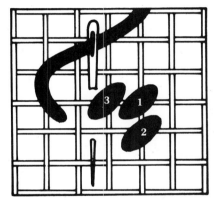

Fourth Stitch

4. Complete the fourth stitch to the left of the third, and bring the needle out in the space just under the third stitch. You are now beginning to work your way down the side of the triangle shape.

Fifth and Sixth Stitches

5. Make the fifth stitch in the same way to the left of the second stitch, bringing the needle out just below it. Complete the sixth stitch under the second, bringing the needle out in the space below the sixth stitch. You have now worked your way down the side of the triangle and are ready to begin working back up the side.

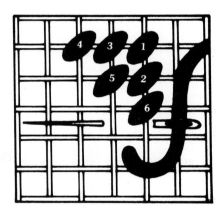

Seventh and Eighth Stitches

6. The seventh stitch is made directly under the sixth, with the needle coming out to the left of the sixth stitch. The eighth stitch is made in the same way to the left of the sixth. Continue working up the side of the triangle, placing the last stitch to the left of the fourth stitch.

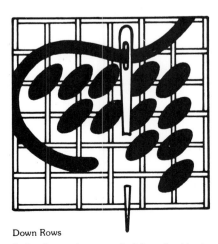

Down Rows

7. On all rows that are worked *down* the side of the triangle, the needle should be plied *vertically* and should be parallel to the threads of the canvas.

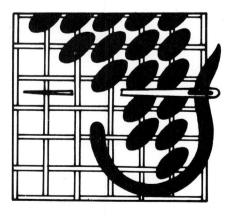

Up Rows

8. On all rows that are worked *up* the side of the triangle, the needle should be plied *horizontally* and should be parallel to the threads of the canvas.

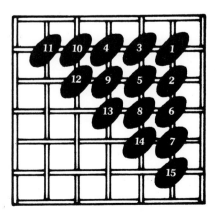

Sequence of Stitches

9. The stitches on all subsequent rows are worked alternately up and down the slanted side of the triangle.

BEGINNING AND ENDING A THREAD

To begin stitching, pass the needle from the back of the canvas to the front, leaving a tail of yarn about an inch and a half long on the underside. Hold the tail in position with one hand under the canvas, securing the yarn in the first five or six stitches. Always trim the excess close to the underside.

You can also begin a thread by knotting the end of the yarn and passing it through the canvas from front to back, and up again to the position of your first stitch. Place the knot about an inch below your starting point. As you stitch, the yarn will be caught and the knot can be snipped off.

Once the work is progressing, new strands of yarn can be started by weaving the end through several stitches on the back of your work. End a thread in the same way, but be careful not to start one thread and end another in the same place. The double thickness will show as a lumpy spot on the front of the work. Instead, secure a new thread at right angles to where the last one was ended. Be careful not to catch any threads of the canvas, or the stitches on the front will be distorted.

If you're working on a frame, you may find it awkward at first to secure the thread without being able to see the underside of your needlepoint. Resist the temptation to flip the piece over. Let yourself become accustomed to guiding the needle with your fingers alone. Soon you will overcome the initial awkwardness and save yourself time and effort.

STITCHING HINTS

The tension of your stitches determines not only the smoothness of your finished piece, but also the amount of distortion. Work with a steady, gentle motion. Don't finish each stitch with a tug. Wool is a resilient live fiber that will even itself out, given time and breathing space. You will find that your stitching suddenly looks better the next day because the wool has relaxed during the night. If the stitches are too tight, the wool will be strained and will stay that way, pulling the canvas badly out of shape.

As the yarn is brought in and out of the canvas, it turns and eventually curls. Twist the needle slightly as you bring each stitch out, keeping the yarn flat and even. Yarn that is twisted makes an unattractive, lumpy stitch.

Ideally, the needle should be brought up through a hole that does not already have a stitch in it, but this is not always possible, especially on pieces that are heavily patterned. When there is no choice but to bring the needle up through a space with a stitch in it, slide the needle through with a slight pressure against the threads of the canvas, tilting the needle away from the stitch. Otherwise the needle will split the yarn, dividing the other stitch into two sections.

You may find that as a patterned area is filled in, it becomes increasingly difficult to bring the needle through the canvas without pulling fibers from the back of the work to the surface. To lessen the problem, trim the finished threads very close so no fraying ends will be left hanging. Keep on hand an extra needle that has been threaded with a short piece of yarn. Poke the needle between the two offending stitches with a quick downward motion, pulling the extraneous fibers to the back of the work.

REPAIRS

Even when you use the greatest care, a few wrong stitches now and then are almost inevitable. Fortunately, most errors can be corrected.

If a few stitches have been worked in the wrong place or the wrong direction and the thread has not yet been secured in the back of your work, simply pull the stitches out, one by one. Don't leave the yarn in your needle. Instead, remove the needle and use it to pry the stitches loose, first in front of the work and then in back. Pull the yarn all the way through to the other side each time.

An error of more than a few stitches must be cut out very carefully with embroidery scissors. Slide the point under one or two stitches and cut, being careful not to catch the threads of the canvas. Stop a few stitches short of where you want to end and pull out the rest with the tip of your needle, until you have a piece long enough to secure in the back. Use a pair of tweezers to pull out the short pieces you've cut.

Should you cut a strand of the canvas, don't despair. Peel off a thread from the edge of a piece of extra canvas, lay it across the broken thread, and stitch over it.

Most of the designs in this book are symmetrical either by quarters or halves. If you should make an error, such as positioning part of a design incorrectly or altering the shape of a motif by a few stitches, consider leaving it rather than correcting it. If the error is repeated throughout the piece, it no longer looks like a mistake, and in fact it isn't. Much of the charm of Oriental rugs is due to the weavers' cleverness in using design elements that appear spontaneously. By making mistakes work for you, you will be approaching your task in much the same spirit as the original designers.

Should an individual error go unnoticed until the work can no longer be corrected, remember that Oriental weavers, believing perfection belongs to Allah alone, often include a deliberate error in their rugs.

USING THE GRAPHS

Elaborate design contributes greatly to the beauty of Oriental rugs. It also contributes greatly to the problems of charting the designs. If all the shapes were to be drawn on the same chart, the result would be a frustrating and confusing mass of symbols that probably could not be deciphered even with the aid of a magnifying glass. Thus, for the following projects, every piece has been separated into a series of graphs, each of which shows only two or three colors.

It is characteristic of Oriental rugs for a single dark color to be used to outline the border areas and the major designs in the field. The first graph of each series shows these outline areas. Once this graph has been worked, the size of the piece and the major shapes will be established.

The second graph in the series will show smaller design areas to be worked in other colors. The areas that were worked from the first graph will show as heavy dots on the second graph. They appear on the second graph only to make it easier to locate the position of areas yet to be worked in relationship to those that have already been stitched. On all subsequent graphs in the series, heavy dots represent areas that have been worked from preceding graphs.

In order to simplify the graphs of heavily patterned designs further, only a few of the very clearest symbols have been used. The same symbols appear on every graph in a series, each time representing a different group of colors.

Remember:
• Heavy dots represent work already completed and are shown only to make it easier to position new work correctly.
• The color code is different on every graph in a series, even though the symbols are the same as those used on the preceding graphs.

Most Oriental designs are symmetrical in quarters or halves —each right-hand quarter or half of the design is a mirror image of that on the left. Therefore, the graphs generally show only the right-hand half or upper right-hand quarter of the design, but they can be matched easily with the other sections of the piece. If you have trouble working the sections of the design not specifically graphed, you can have your local printer make a flopped photostat of the graph, to show the opposite side.

The center lines of stitches in each piece are marked with double bars at the outer edge of the graph. Work the stitches in these center lines only once.

The border designs in some pieces reverse direction at the center point. It is important that in these pieces you do not continue the pattern in the same direction across the entire border or the corners will not meet properly. When the direction does not change in the middle, the graph will show the pattern that is to be repeated all the way across each side of the border.

Several rows of solid color frame each design. This final border is not shown on the graphs, but instructions for it are found in the text.

Remember that when you work designs from graphs, the graph's grid lines do *not* correspond to the horizontal and vertical threads of your canvas. Rather, each square on the graph represents a finished stitch as it appears on your piece of needlepoint. You should think of the graph's grid lines as outlines of the finished stitches on your needlepoint.

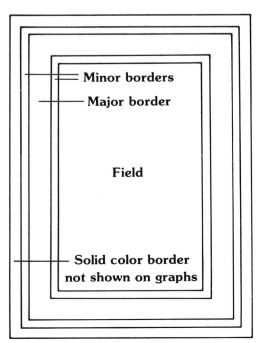

Minor borders
Major border
Field
Solid color border not shown on graphs

Laver Kerman

Paternayan Color	Number	Full 66" Strands
Red	200	165
White	001	50
Yellow	447	53
Blue	733	67
Dk Blue	365	130

Yarn: 2 Ply
Canvas Gauge: 12 Mesh
Canvas Size: 32" × 42¾"
Finished Size: 26" × 36¾"

Note: The graphs for this piece show the right-hand half of the design. To make certain the piece is positioned correctly on the canvas, work the row of blue that surrounds the entire field before beginning the design. Then measure from the outside of the blue line to the outer edge of the canvas. There should be 5¼" on each side for the border, and another 3" on each side to be left unworked.

Begin working the design at the top of the field and work toward the bottom. Fill in the red background after the entire design is completed. Work the background in the basket-weave stitch, starting at the upper right and working diagonally toward the lower left.

18

Graph 1

■ Work solid areas in red.
▨ Work slashed areas in yellow.
◪ Work triangles in blue.

Fill in all remaining areas in white.

19

Graph 2
The dots represent the bottom row worked from Graph 1.

■ Work solid areas in red.
▨ Work slashed areas in yellow.
◩ Work triangles in blue.

Fill in all remaining areas in white.

20

Graph 3

The dots represent the bottom row worked from Graph 2.

■ Work solid areas in red.
☑ Work slashed areas in yellow.
◪ Work triangles in blue.

Fill in all remaining areas in white.

21

Graph 4

The dots represent the blue line around the field worked from Graphs 1, 2, and 3.

■ Work solid areas in white.
☑ Work slashed areas in blue.

The center of the second full motif on the top and bottom border should coincide with the vertical center line of the field.

The center of the third full motif on the side borders should coincide with the horizontal center line of the field. There will be a total of three full motifs on the top and bottom border, and five full motifs on the side borders, plus four corner motifs.

Graph 5

The dots represent work completed from Graph 4.

■ Work solid areas in dark blue.
☑ Work slashed areas in yellow.

Using the color photo (Plate 2) as a guide, fill in the background of the major border in red. Next, add one row of blue around the entire piece, and then an additional 5 rows of dark blue all around.

23

Heriz

Paternayan Color	Number	Full 66" Strands
Red	242	135
White	005	85
Yellow	445	49
Pink	860	18
Blue	731	59
Dk Blue	321	126

Yarn: 2 Ply
Canvas Gauge: 12 Mesh
Canvas Size: 31½" Square
Pattern Area Size: 25½" Square
Box Cushion Depth: 2¼"

Note: The graphs for this piece can be turned clockwise to work all four quarters of the design. The yarn count allows for 28 border rows of dark blue, which are necessary for a box cushion. For a pillow, purchase only 73 strands of dark blue yarn and work 12 border rows.

24

Graph 1

■ Work solid areas in yellow.
☑ Work slashed areas in red.

25

Graph 2

The dots represent work completed from Graph 1.

■ Work solid areas in white.
☑ Work slashed areas in red.

Graph 3

The dots represent work completed from Graphs 1 and 2.

■ Work solid areas in bright blue.
◤ Work triangles in pink.

27

Graph 4
The dots represent work completed from Graphs 1, 2, and 3.

■ Work solid areas in red.
☑ Work slashed areas in dark blue.

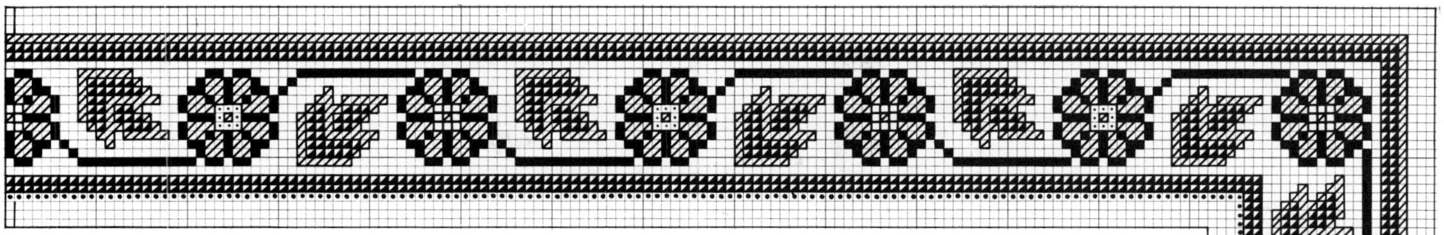

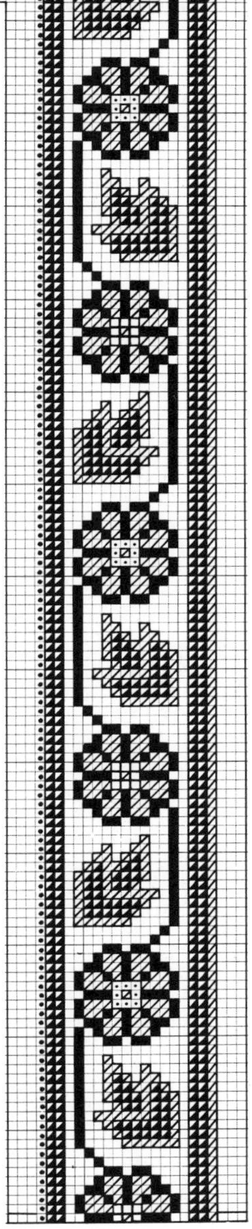

Graph 5

The large dots represent the outer row of red surrounding the field, which has already been completed.

■ Work solid areas in yellow.
☑ Work slashed areas in red.
◪ Work triangles in white.
□ Work outlined areas in bright blue.
⊡ Work small dot in pink.

Fill in the background in bright blue. For a box cushion, work 28 rows of dark blue straight out from each side. Do not work corners. (See Plate 3.) For a pillow, work 12 rows of dark blue around the entire piece.

Kashan

Paternayan Color	Number	Full 66" Strands
Rose	232	56
White	014	113
Yellow	467	10
Turquoise	793	38
Blue	355	36

Yarn: 2 Ply
Canvas Gauge: 12 Mesh
Canvas Size: 24½" × 31"
Finished Size: 18½" × 25"

Note: Use the graphs for this piece to work the upper right-hand and lower left-hand quarters of the design.

Graph 1

■ Work solid areas in blue.

31

Graph 2
The dots represent work completed from Graph 1.

■ Work solid areas in white.
☑ Work slashed areas in yellow.

32

Graph 3

The dots represent work completed from Graphs 1 and 2.

■ Work solid areas in rose.

Using Plate 5 as a guide, fill in the background of the round motifs in the major border with white. Then work the background of the major border in turquoise.

33

Graph 4   The dots represent work com-
pleted from Graphs 1, 2, and 3.   ■ Work solid areas in turquoise.

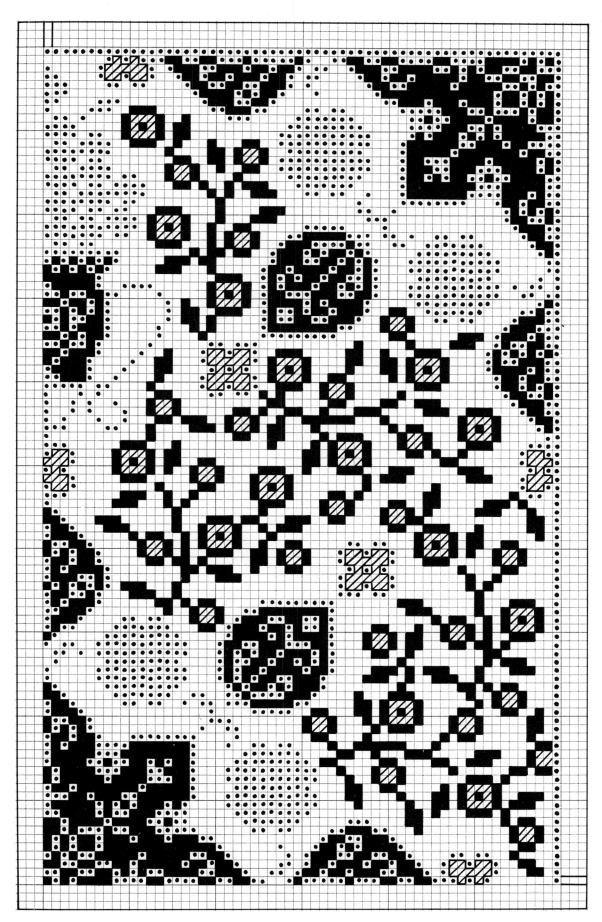

Graph 5

The dots represent work completed from Graphs 1, 2, 3, and 4.

■ Work solid areas in rose.
▨ Work slashed areas in yellow.

Using Plate 5 as a guide, fill in the background of the field and minor borders in white. Work 10 rows of white around the entire piece.

Tree and Garden

Paternayan Color	Number	Full 66" Strands
Red	845	67
White	010	25
Gold	453	61
Pink	289	41
Green	532	17
Turquoise	318	25
Dk Blue	740	73

Yarn: 2 Ply
Canvas Gauge: 12 Mesh
Canvas Size: 22½" × 39"
Finished Size: 16½" × 33"

Note: Use the graphs for this piece to stitch the upper right-hand and lower left-hand quarters of the design.

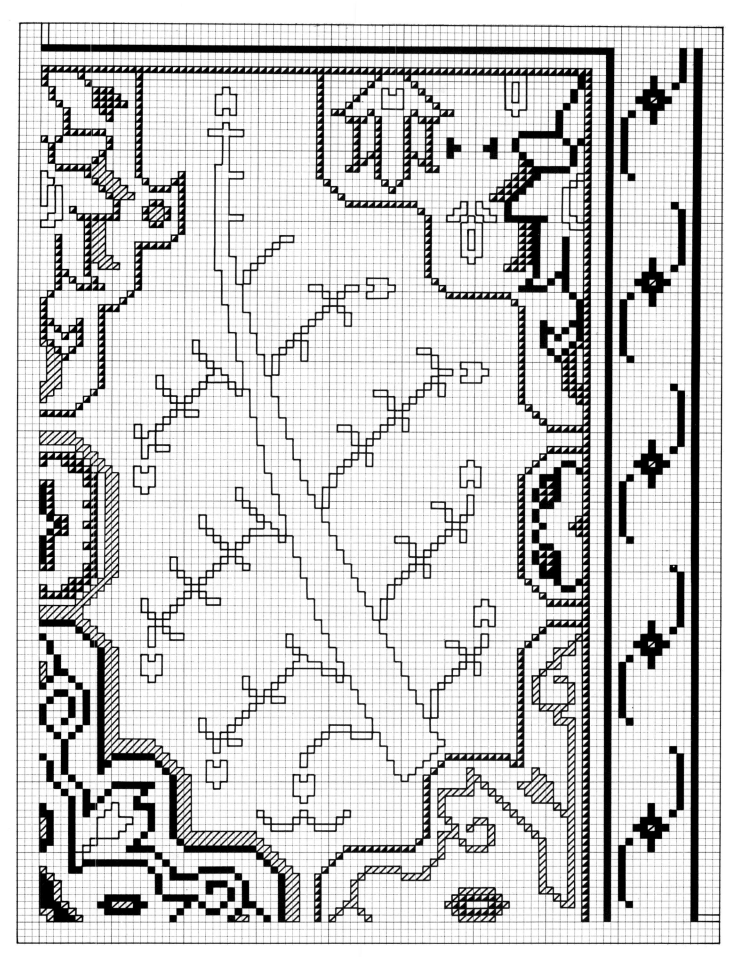

Graph 1 ■ Work solid areas in dark blue. ◩ Work triangles in turquoise.
          ▨ Work slashed areas in gold. □ Work outlined areas in green.

Graph 2 The dots represent work completed from Graph 1.

■ Work solid areas in red.
☑ Work slashed areas in white.

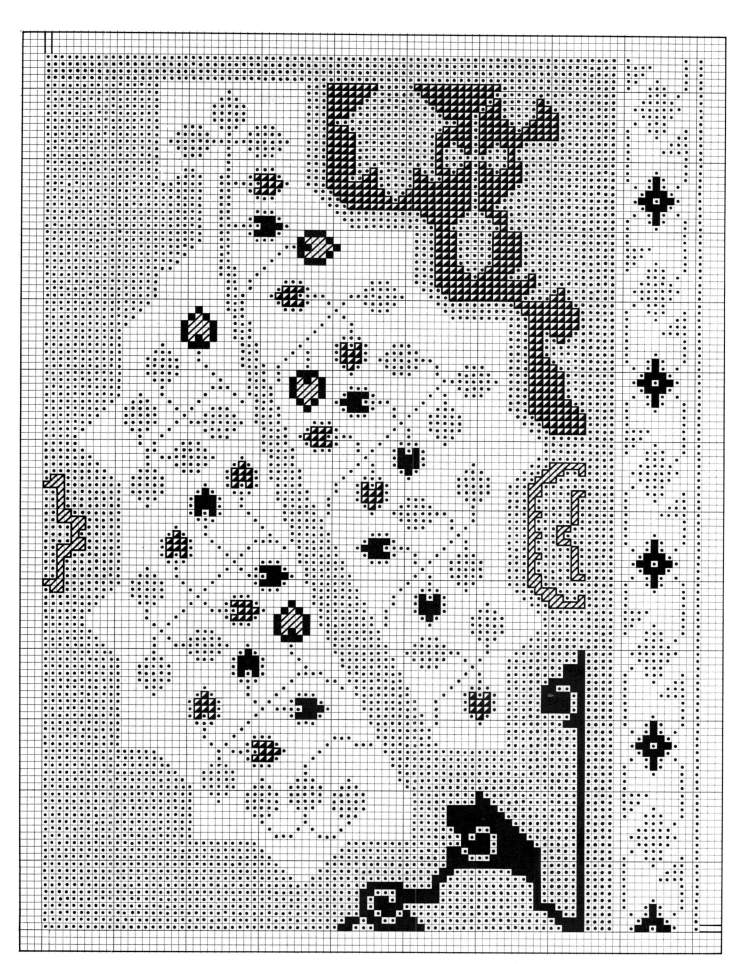

Graph 3   The dots represent work completed from Graphs 1 and 2.

■ Work solid areas in turquoise.
◪ Work slashed areas in pink.
◪ Work triangles in gold.

Graph 4 (above)

The dots represent the top line completed from Graphs 1, 2, and 3.

■ Work solid areas in dark blue.
☑ Work slashed areas in white.
◪ Work triangles in turquoise.

Graph 5 (below)

The dots represent work completed from Graph 4.

■ Work solid areas in red.
☑ Work slashed areas in green.

Graph 6

The dots represent work completed from Graphs 4 and 5.

■ Work solid areas in gold.
☑ Work slashed areas in pink.
◩ Work triangles in white.

Using Plate 7 as a guide, fill in the background of the flower field in dark blue. Fill in the background of the border in gold. Add 2 rows of red around the entire piece, and then work an additional 7 rows of pink all around.

41

Luristan

Paternayan Color	Number	Full 66" Strands
Orange	958	75
White	001	25
Yellow	457	29
Blue	731	31
Dk Blue	321	88

Yarn: 2 Ply
Canvas Gauge: 12 Mesh
Canvas Size: 29" × 26¼"
Finished Size: 23" × 20¼"

Note: The graphs show the right-hand half of the design. Do not reverse the direction of the birds in the border at the halfway point. Continue working in the established pattern, keeping all the birds facing the top.

Graph 1

■ Work solid areas in orange.
☒ Work slashed areas in blue.

Graph 2
The dots represent work completed from Graph 1.

■ Work solid areas in yellow.
◪ Work triangles in white.

Graph 3

The dots represent work completed from Graphs 1 and 2.

■ Work solid areas in dark blue.

▨ Work slashed areas in blue.

◪ Work triangles in white.

Using Plate 9 as a guide, fill in the background of the major border in orange. Then work 8 rows of dark blue around the entire piece.

Yuntdag

Paternayan Color	Number	Full 66" Strands
Red	213	58
Off-white	011	41
Yellow	400	30
Orange	958	37
Lavender	618	86
Green	545	26
Blue Grey	308	73

Yarn: 3 Ply
Canvas Gauge: 10 Mesh
Canvas Size: 29" Square
Finished Size: 23" Square

Graph 1

■ Work solid areas in yellow.
☑ Work slashed areas in red.
◪ Work triangles in off-white.

Graph 2

For upper-right quarter and lower-left quarter. To work lower left, turn graph clockwise. The dots represent work completed from Graph 1.

■ Work solid areas in blue grey.
☑ Work slashed areas in red.

Graph 3

For upper-left quarter and lower-right quarter. To work lower right, turn graph clockwise. The dots represent work completed from Graphs 1 and 2.

■ Work solid areas in blue grey.
☑ Work slashed areas in red.

Graph 4

For upper-right quarter and lower-left quarter. To work lower left, turn graph clockwise. The dots represent work completed from Graphs 1, 2, and 3.

■ Work solid areas in lavender.
◪ Work slashed areas in yellow.
◪ Work triangles in off-white.
□ Work outlined squares in green.

50

Graph 5

For upper-left quarter and lower-right quarter. To work lower right, turn graph clockwise. The dots represent work completed from Graphs 1, 2, 3, and 4.

■ Work solid areas in lavender.
☑ Work slashed areas in yellow.
◪ Work triangles in off-white.
☐ Work outlined squares in green.

Work 10 rows of lavender around the entire piece.

51

Kazak

Paternayan Color	Number	Full 66" Strands
Red	845	90
White	010	64
Yellow	457	21
Green	532	55
Blue	741	55
Rust	201	42

Yarn: 3 Ply
Canvas Gauge: 10 Mesh
Canvas Size: 26" × 32"
Finished Size: 20" × 26"

Note: Use the graphs for this piece to work the upper right-hand and lower left-hand quarters, except for the center medallion, which must be worked as shown on Graph 2.

Graph 1   ■ Work solid areas in blue.
             ▨ Work slashed areas in rust.
             ◤ Work triangles in green.

53

Graph 2 The dots represent work completed from Graph 1.

■ Work solid areas in red.
◩ Work slashed areas in yellow.

Using Plate 13 as a guide, fill in all remaining areas in white. Then work 6 rows of green around the entire piece.

Ezine

Paternayan Color	Number	Full 66" Strands
Red	242	50
White	010	32
Yellow	447	19
Blue	740	67

Yarn: 3 Ply
Canvas Gauge: 10 Mesh
Canvas Size: 22" Square
Finished Size: 16" Square

Note: Use the graphs for this piece to work the upper right-hand and lower left-hand quarters of the design. If the piece is used on a bunching table, only 3 border rows are needed. For a pillow, purchase 25 additional strands of blue yarn and work a total of 8 border rows.

Graph 1

■ Work solid areas in blue.
◪ Work triangles in red.

Graph 2

The dots represent work completed from Graph 1.

■ Work solid areas in yellow.
☑ Work slashed areas in red.
◪ Work triangles in white.

Using Plate 15 as a guide, work the remaining background areas in blue. Then work 2 additional rows of blue around the entire piece for the bunching table, and 7 additional rows for a pillow.

Bakhtiari

Paternayan Color	Number	Full 66" Strands
Rust	952	36
Green	553	35
White	010	51
Blue	386	44
Dk Blue	334	23

Yarn: 2 Ply
Canvas Gauge: 12 Mesh
Canvas Size: 24½″ Square
Finished Size: 18½″ Square

Note: Work the 9 compartment designs so that the top faces the same direction in each one. Work the vase design in the 4 corner squares, and the willow design in the center compartment of each outer series of 3 squares.

Graph 1

■ Work solid areas in rust.
▨ Work slashed areas in dark blue.

59

Graph 2

The dots represent work completed from Graph 1.

■ Work solid areas in green.

Graph 3

The dots represent work completed from Graphs 1 and 2.

■ Work solid areas in the lighter blue.

▨ Work triangles in white.

Using Plate 18 as a guide, fill in the background of each compartment and the border in white. Then work 10 rows of the lighter blue around the entire piece.

Sejshour

Paternayan Color	Number	Full 66" Strands
Orange	960	59
White	010	19
Yellow	457	45
Peach	988	38
Green	508	9
Dk Blue	365	71

Yarn: 2 Ply

Canvas Gauge: 12 Mesh

Canvas Size: 26¼" Square

Finished Size: 20¼" Square

Note: The graphs for the upper right-hand quarter of the field can be turned clockwise to work the other 3 quarters. The border design is worked straight across as shown.

Graph 1

■ Work solid areas in yellow.
◨ Work slashed areas in orange.

Graph 2

The dots represent work completed from Graph 1.

■ Work solid areas in dark blue.

Graph 3

The dots represent work completed from Graphs 1 and 2.

■ Work solid areas in green.
◩ Work triangles in white.

Using Plate 19 as a guide, fill in the remaining background of the field in yellow.

Graph 4

The dots represent the dark blue row surrounding the field.

■ Work solid areas in dark blue.
☑ Work slashed areas in yellow.
◪ Work triangles in peach.

Work border design as shown until there are 14 Running Dog patterns on each side of the square.

Graph 5

The dots represent work completed from Graph 4.

■ Work solid areas in orange.
☑ Work slashed areas in white.
◪ Work triangles in dark blue.

Work 9 rows of peach around the entire piece.

Gendje I

Paternayan Color	Number	Full 66" Strands
Rose	238	85
Yellow	437	41
Green	510	66
Dk Green	506	81

Yarn: 3 Ply
Canvas Gauge: 10 Mesh
Canvas Size: 26½" Square
Finished Size: 20½" Square

Note: Use the graphs to work the upper right-hand and lower left-hand quarters of the design. Do not reverse the direction of the border design at the halfway point. Continue working the border in the same direction all the way across.

Graph 1

■ Work solid areas in the lighter green.

☑ Work slashed areas in rose.

◪ Work triangles in dark green.

Graph 2

The dots represent work completed from Graph 1.

■ Work solid areas in yellow.
☑ Work slashed areas in rose.
◪ Work triangles in the lighter green.

Using Plate 20 as a guide, fill in the background of the center medallion and the outer field in dark green. Then fill in the background of the border in rose, and work 8 rows of the lighter green around the entire piece.

70

Gendje II

Paternayan Color	Number	Full 66" Strands
Red	242	50
White	005	20
Yellow	402	25
Lt Blue	743	9
Dk Blue	721	54

Yarn: 2 Ply
Canvas Gauge: 12 Mesh
Canvas Size: 22¾" Square
Finished Size: 16¾" Square

Graph 1

■ Work solid areas in red.
☑ Work slashed areas in dark blue.
◩ Work triangles in white.

Graph 2

The dots represent work completed from Graph 1.

- ■ Work solid areas in yellow.
- ◪ Work slashed areas in light blue.
- ◪ Work triangles in white.

Using Plate 21 as a guide, work the background of the stripes. Starting in the upper-left corner, fill in the first stripe with yellow, the second stripe with dark blue, and the third stripe with red. Follow this sequence 3 times until the entire field is filled in.

73

Graph 3

The dots represent the outer row of dark blue, which was completed from Graph 1. The graphs for the borders can be turned clockwise to work the other 3 corners.

■ Work solid areas in dark blue.
☑ Work slashed areas in yellow.

74

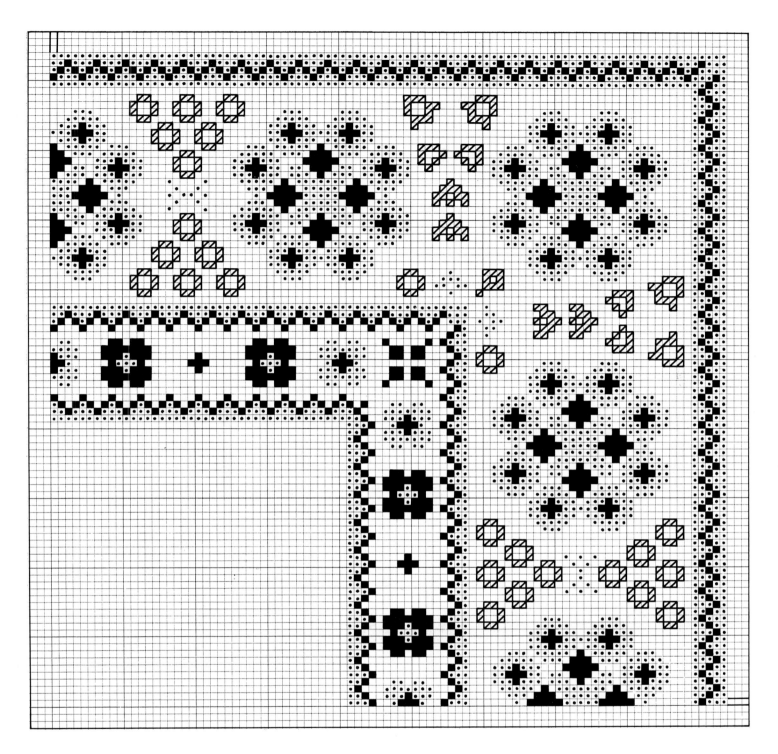

Graph 4

The dots represent work completed from Graph 3.

■ Work solid areas in red.
▨ Work slashed areas in light blue.

75

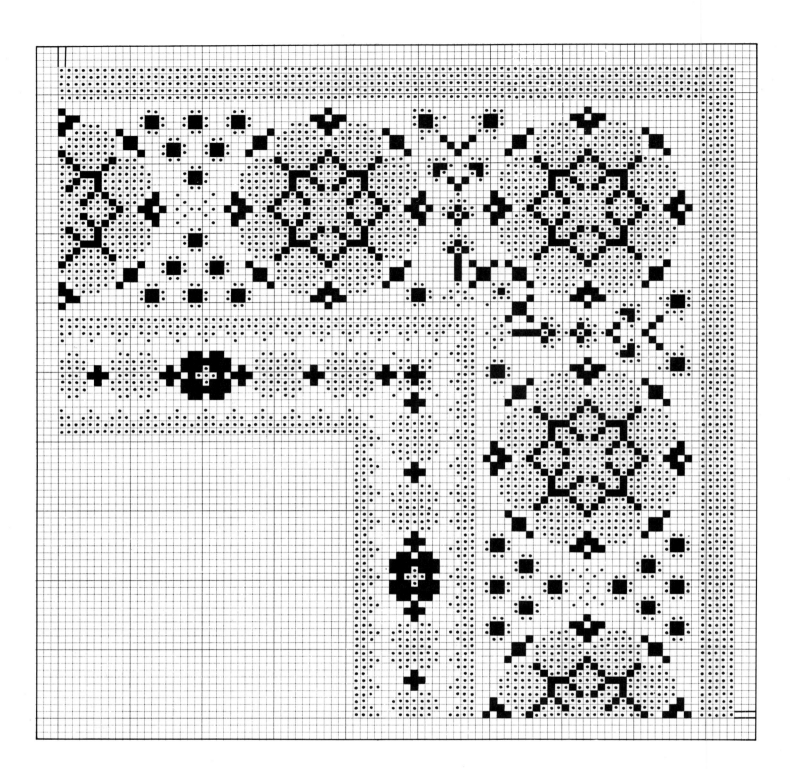

Graph 5

The dots represent work completed from Graphs 3 and 4.

■ Work solid areas in white.

Using Plate 21 as a guide, fill in the background of the minor border in dark blue and the background of the major border in red. Then work 7 additional rows of dark blue around the entire piece.

76

Derbend

Paternayan Color	Number	Full 66" Strands
Red	242	39
White	005	11
Lt Orange	970	23
Blue	733	45
Dk Blue	305	69

Yarn: 3 Ply
Canvas Gauge: 10 Mesh
Canvas Size: 23½" Square
Finished Size: 17½" Square

Note: Use the graphs for this piece to work the upper right-hand and lower left-hand quarters of the design.

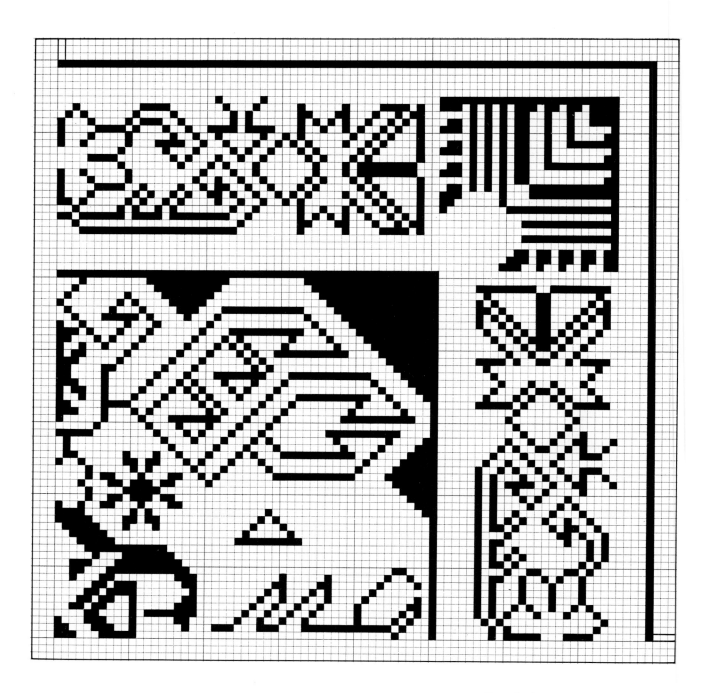

Graph 1

■ Work solid areas in dark blue.

Graph 2

The dots represent work completed from Graph 1.

- ■ Work solid areas in red.
- ☑ Work slashed areas in light orange.
- ◪ Work triangles in white.

Using Plate 22 as a guide, fill in all remaining areas in the lighter blue. Then work 7 additional rows of dark blue around the entire piece.

Karabagh

Paternayan Color	Number	Full 66" Strands
Red	242	91
White	005	59
Yellow	437	5
Turquoise	755	14
Olive	553	7
Dk Green	504	10
Black	050	49

Yarn: 3 Ply
Canvas Gauge: 10 Mesh
Canvas Size: 25" Square
Finished Size: 19" Square

Note: Use the graphs for this piece to work the upper right-hand and lower left-hand quarters of the design.

Graph 1

■ Work solid areas in black.

Graph 2

The dots represent work completed from Graph 1.

■ Work solid areas in red.
☑ Work slashed areas in dark green.

82

Graph 3

The dots represent work completed from Graphs 1 and 2.

■ Work solid areas in turquoise.
◩ Work slashed areas in yellow.
◪ Work triangles in olive.

Using Plate 23 as a guide, work the field background in red. Then fill in all remaining areas in white, and work 8 rows of red around the entire piece.

Chila

Paternayan Color	Number	Full 66" Strands
Red	242	38
White	010	54
Yellow	453	11
Blue	318	62
Dk Blue	365	40

Yarn: 3 Ply
Canvas Gauge: 10 Mesh
Canvas Size: 24" × 23"
Finished Size: 18" × 17"

Graph 1

■ Work solid areas in red.

▨ Work slashed areas in white.

◩ Work triangles in the lighter blue.

Graph 2

The dots represent work completed from Graph 1.

- ■ Work solid areas in dark blue.
- ▨ Work slashed areas in red.
- ◪ Work triangles in yellow.

Graph 3

The dots represent work completed from Graphs 1 and 2.

■ Work solid areas in the lighter blue.

☑ Work slashed areas in yellow.

◪ Work triangles in white.

Using Plate 24 as a guide, fill in the background of the 2 minor borders in white. Then work 8 rows of the lighter blue around the entire piece.

BLOCKING AND FINISHING

Proper blocking is an essential step in producing a beautiful piece of needlepoint. Because of the diagonal pull of the stitches, some distortion of the canvas is inevitable. If the piece has been worked on a frame, a single blocking should suffice to bring it into shape. Needlepoint that has been worked on your lap may require two or three blockings, especially if the piece is large.

Blocking can be done professionally at most needlepoint stores and upholsterers. For a single piece, it may be worth the expense, but I don't know anyone who ever stopped at a single piece. The best idea is to assume that if this is your first effort, it is only the first of many. Learn to block the needlepoint yourself and you not only spare the expense, but you can also be certain the finished result is exactly to your liking.

Materials

Wallboard is sometimes used as a blocking board, but I find that a piece of plywood a half inch thick works best. Your local lumberyard can cut it to the size you need. Give one side of the board a coat or two of wood sealer, so the wet needlepoint can be stapled on it without the wood swelling from absorbing water. If your stitches are very even, the piece can be blocked with the right side up. However, if the stitches are a little irregular, the piece should be blocked with the right side facing the board. The pressure will flatten the stitches slightly so they lie more evenly next to each other. If you plan to block your needlepoint facedown, cover the board with an old sheet or a piece of white muslin to protect the surface of your work. Staple the sheet or muslin all around the edge of the board, pulling it as tight as possible. Trim off the excess, and then wet the cloth on the board with warm water to shrink it slightly.

It is often recommended that a grid pattern of two-inch squares be drawn with indelible markers on the board or cloth covering in order to facilitate squaring the work. I find that on large pieces with a three-inch edge of canvas, this doesn't work very well. The outer edge of the canvas can be absolutely straight, while the edge of the needlepoint itself can still be crooked. Therefore, I don't worry about lining up the outer edge with a grid. I square the edges of the needlepoint with a large plastic triangle, carried by most art suppliers, and I am not concerned about the shape of the canvas outside the work.

The needlepoint canvas can be fastened to the board with tacks, but a heavy-duty staple gun is much faster and easier to work with. You will need a large supply of one-quarter-inch staples, preferably rust-free. Get a sturdy staple remover with a prong at the end for prying the staples loose.

Stretching the Canvas

Before you begin stretching the canvas, take it to the sink and wet it with cool water. Use a sponge or a terry washcloth and dab the water into the canvas with a downward motion rather than a sideways motion. Rubbing the water into the wool instead of patting it can cause the colors to bleed and can shift the stitches out of shape. Don't mix vinegar with the water to set the colors. Modern dyeing methods make it unnecessary.

When the canvas is wet all the way through, gently squeeze it to remove the most obvious excess water and then roll it in a towel to remove the remaining excess. Use a white or pastel towel rather than a colored or patterned one that might bleed onto your work.

Your needlepoint should now be uniformly damp and pliable. You will notice a definite slant to the piece. If you measure diagonally each way from corner to corner, you will find that one of the two measurements is shorter than the other. Hold the canvas firmly on either end of the short measurement and pull until the shape of the canvas is nearly square and the two diagonal measurements are nearly equal.

Stapling

You are now ready to attach the needlepoint to the blocking board. Have on hand your staple gun, plastic triangle, a tape measure, and the one-quarter-inch staples. Put your canvas on the board, and place your triangle on one corner of the needlepoint (not on the edge of the canvas). Pull your needlepoint into line with the two straight sides of the triangle, and staple the canvas one-half to one-quarter inch from the edge of your needlepoint. If your staples are not rust-free, stay far enough away from the edge to prevent any rust from touching the needlepoint. Be generous with your staples, placing them very close together so the strain of pulling the other corners into shape won't distort your first corner.

You now have one square corner as a guide for positioning the rest of the canvas. Using the dimensions of the finished piece given in the instructions, measure each side and pull it until it reaches the proper length. Staple the remaining corners lightly. Now measure the two diagonals again and adjust the sides until the two dimensions are equal. Next, square each corner as you did the first. Staple close to the needlepoint all the way around.

Drying

Dry your needlepoint horizontally. Placing it vertically can cause the colors to bleed as the water works its way down the piece.

Do not place the board near heat to accelerate drying. Let it dry naturally in a ventilated area at room temperature. You will find that when the piece is dry, it will be rather stiff because some of the dissolved sizing remains in the wool. The piece may also buckle slightly as it dries. This should cause no concern, as the piece straightens out again when it is steamed.

Steaming

Steaming the needlepoint restores the plumpness of the stitches and straightens any buckling that may have occurred as it dried. If the piece has been blocked with the right side up, place it with the right side down on a fluffy terry-cloth towel. Hold the steam iron against the back of the work, but don't press down. If the needlepoint was blocked face-down, steam it with the right side up, holding the iron about two or three inches above the surface.

Finishing

Before the excess canvas is trimmed off, the edge where the needlepoint and the canvas meet should be secured. Otherwise the canvas threads will loosen and the backing won't hold. The quickest way to do this is to run two or three rows of machine stitching, about one-quarter inch apart, close to the edge of the needlepoint. A better way is to stitch straight seam binding right against the edge of the needle-point. Stitch two rows about one-eighth inch apart, turning the corners by folding them. This makes a good firm edge, and the piece won't fall apart later.

If you are making the pieces into pillows, you can back them yourself, but I really feel that after all the time invested in your needlepoint it should be turned over to a professional for the final touch. Most needlepoint stores offer this service, but an upholsterer will usually charge less. To him, a piece of needlepoint is the same as any other fabric.

Choose a fairly substantial backing material, such as cotton velvet or heavy silk. The color preferably should match one of the minor colors in the piece. If one of the major colors is used, the effect tends to be too gaudy.

Cording makes a handsome finishing touch, though I don't recommend making your own. I find that with my sewing machine I have difficulty handling the extra layers of heavy material together with the needlepoint. An upholsterer can do a far more successful job. Keep the cording the same color and fabric as the backing. A plain backing without cording also looks attractive, since all the designs have a patterned border framed by a solid color.

Should you decide to finish the piece yourself, cut the backing five-eighths inch larger than the needlepoint all around. Pin the two pieces together, right sides facing, and stitch directly into the first row of needlepoint, using the zipper foot on your machine. Leave four or five inches un-worked along one side and turn the pillow right side out through this opening. When the pillow has been stuffed, care-fully sew the opening together by hand.

The stuffing can be put directly into the pillow, but it is much better to place it in a casing that can be removed when the pillow needs cleaning. Commercial foam pillow forms are also available, but they tend to be rather stiff. Moreover, since the pillows vary so greatly in size, finding a form that fits your piece may be a problem. However, making your own casing is a fairly simple matter. Cut two pieces of muslin or heavy cotton the same size as your backing. Stitch a five-eighths-inch seam all the way around, leaving an opening of a few inches along one side, as you did on the pillow. Turn the casing right side out, and stuff it with a polyester or feather filling. Old nylons cut into shreds also make an excellent filling. Close the opening either by hand or machine.

Needlepoint pieces can also be finished flat, for use as wall hangings or table runners. A heavy cotton velvet upholstery fabric with foam backing works best, giving the piece the weight it needs to hang or lie properly.

1. Cut four strips of fabric one and one-quarter inch wider than the finished width of the edging, and at least one and one-quarter inch longer than the finished length. See Figure 1. With right sides facing, and allowing a five-eighths-inch seam, stitch the strips to the four sides of the needlepoint, ending where the needlepoint ends. Do not stitch beyond this point. Open up the piece and press the seams from the wrong side until the work lies flat.

2. Place the edge of a forty-five-degree plastic triangle five-eighths inch away from the end of the stitching and cut along the slanted line. See Figure 2. Holding the slanted ends with right sides facing, stitch each corner together, working from the corner of the needlepoint to the outside edge of the strip. When all four corners have been stitched, press the seams from the wrong side until the piece is flat. Use a damp cloth if necessary.

3. Cut a piece of backing the same dimensions as the outside measurements of the strips surrounding the needle-point. See Figure 3. Placing the two pieces right side together, stitch all the way around, allowing a five-eighths-inch seam. Leave several inches unworked and pull the piece right side out through this opening, after pressing the seams open on the wrong side. Sew the opening together by hand.

If the needlepoint is to be framed, it should be blocked and mounted either on a one-quarter-inch chipboard or on a stretcher frame. A thin acid-free ragboard should be placed between the needlepoint and the board or frame to protect the work. Chipboard and wood have an acid action that can gradually affect the wool, weakening the fibers and yellowing the colors. If the needlepoint is stapled to the board, make certain the staples are rust-free. Smaller pieces can be secured by pulling the edge of the canvas around to the back of the board and lacing the ends together with a needle and heavy thread. I prefer securing the piece by stapling, how-ever, so it can't shift.

A framed needlework may be covered by glass, but, if you hang it in a protected spot, you may prefer to leave it exposed so the full beauty of your efforts can be enjoyed.

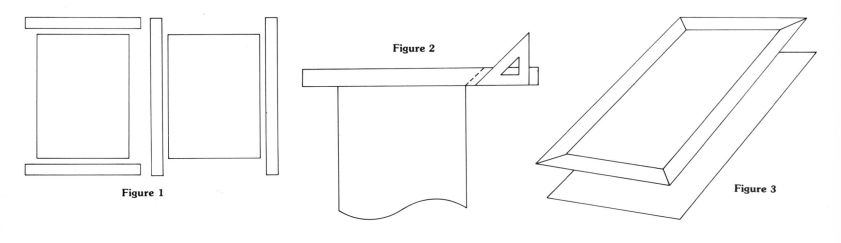

Figure 1   Figure 2   Figure 3

BIBLIOGRAPHY

Arts Council of Great Britain. *Islamic Carpets from the Collection of Joseph V. McMullan.* London: Arts Council of Great Britain, 1972.

Bennett, Ian. *Book of Oriental Carpets and Rugs.* London: Hamlyn Publishing Group Ltd., 1972.

Eiland, Murray L. *Oriental Rugs.* 2nd ed. Boston: New York Graphic Society, 1976.

Gans-Ruedin, E. *The Connoisseur's Guide to Oriental Carpets.* Rutland, Vt.: Charles E. Tuttle Company, 1971.

Gregorian, Arthur T. *Oriental Rugs and the Stories They Tell.* 2nd ed. New York: Charles Scribner's Sons, 1977.

Herbert, Janice Summers. *Oriental Rugs, the Illustrated Guide.* New York: Macmillan Publishing Co., Inc., 1978.

Iten-Maritz, J. *Turkish Carpets.* New York: Harper & Row Publishers, Inc., 1977.

Izmidlian, Georges. *Oriental Rugs and Carpets Today.* Vancouver: Douglas David & Charles Ltd., 1977.

Liebetrau, Preben. *Oriental Rugs in Colour.* New York: Macmillan Publishing Co., Inc., 1963.

Reed, Stanley. *All Color Book of Oriental Carpets and Rugs.* New York: Crescent Books, 1972.

Schurmann, Ulrich. *Caucasian Rugs.* Accokeek, Md.: Washington International Associates, 1964.

Tschebull, Raoul. *Kazak, Carpets of the Caucasus.* New York: The Near Eastern Art Research Center, Inc., 1971.